Channeling
Harrison

Books by David Young

Divine Inner Guidance

Channeling
Harrison

book one
david young

RAINBOW RIDGE
BOOKS

Cover art by Patty Ray (Macca) Avalon
Cover and Interior design by Frame25 Productions
Cover art © Patty Ray Avalon

Published by:
Rainbow Ridge Books, LLC
140 Rainbow Ridge Road
Faber, Virginia 22938
434-361-1723

If you are unable to order this book from your local
bookseller, you may order directly from the distributor.

Square One Publishers, Inc.
115 Herricks Road
Garden City Park, NY 11040
Phone: (516) 535-2010
Fax: (516) 535-2014
Toll-free: 877-900-BOOK

Visit the author at:
www.davidyoungmusic.com

Library of Congress Cataloging-in-Publication Data applied for.

ISBN 978-1-937907-1-22-8

10 9 8 7 6 5 4 3 2 1

Printed on acid-free paper in United States

"One person can make a difference."
—Sandy G.

Editor's Preface

by Robert S. Friedman

I've been involved with some, shall we say, intriguing authors and books in my almost forty years in the publishing business. Authors like Neale Donald Walsch (*Conversations with God*) and Richard Bach (*Messiah's Handbook*) are among them. I must say that working with David Young on *Channeling Harrison* is high on that list. The sheer number of synchronicities that have occurred in his life around his interaction with George Harrison is mind-boggling. Carl Jung, are you listening?

Even in the short time he was at my home in Virginia, as we made the final editing changes, some amazing things happened right here in the house, and in my life. Well before we even contracted the book, stuff was happening around the publishing company. A couple of events are in this book . . . for example, David's meeting on the road, at random, with one of my neighbors (there are only about twelve houses on this entire dead-end unpaved road). The neighbor is a sound engineer, and he just "happened" to have a good friend who was a well-known drummer, and played with George on his album, *All Things Must Pass.*

But I think it's important to mention one incident that didn't make the final cut. While David was here, we had a couple conversations, the theme of which could be summed up as, "What does George *want?*" How did he know that it was really George Harrison, and if so, why was he playing in David's life? I was writing that question on the computer, in the working manuscript, as we wondered how it would be answered. At the exact moment I typed that line, the power went off in the entire house, on a perfectly clear, windless day. And when it came back on in about ten seconds, that line was missing when we booted up the computer and pulled the manuscript back onto the screen. Guess George didn't want us to deal with *that* question right then.

Certainly, George's influence has caused David to write music that pulled him back to his rock roots, and to again write song lyrics, which he had given up writing years ago in order to focus on his flute music. Was George just trying to write "through" David, to express his creativity again in a physical universe? That wouldn't be an unknown or even an unusual phenomenon, as there have been a number of reports of people channeling Beethoven or Bach, and writing some remarkable music in the process. But that music will never be taken seriously as the work of those masters in this material world. After all, how does one *know* it's really Ludwig or Johann Sebastian?

Is George attempting, through David, to get some messages out to the world? Surely he must know that most people might think the whole idea of that notion is just crazy. But perhaps that's the real motivation. If one could somehow *prove* that it's really George, by the sheer number of synchronicities and information that is conveyed . . . then it follows that we would have to accept the reality of life after death. Not necessarily in a "heaven" or a "hell," but that some portion of us, our soul, our essence, our piece of God, lives on and maintains something of our previous personality.

In my humble opinion, I believe that may be the overarching message of this book. Just imagine how the current paradigm of the world would change if human beings *knew*, not just had faith, that life goes on after we shed these bodies . . . that we continue evolving beyond this physical lifetime. Would we treat each other as if we are all brothers and sisters sharing one world—and hold all life sacred? Would we finally understand that love is all you *really* need? I hope that David's adventure of *Channeling Harrison* can help us to understand that universal question. It may be a long and winding road, but I know we'll all get there in the end.

Table of Contents

Prologue: Legend xiii

Chapter 1: 1973 1

Chapter 2: October 2010 4

Chapter 3: This Change Is Gonna Do Me Good 6

Chapter 4: En Route to the Ashram 9

Chapter 5: The Flute and Krishna's Birthday 15

Chapter 6: I Sure Have Seen Better Days 18

Chapter 7: The Concert for Bangladesh 23

Chapter 8: The Online Dating Adventures 29

Chapter 9: Yogaphoria 33

Chapter 10: One Look 36

Chapter 11: Come Home with Me 38

Chapter 12: Whatever Road You Choose 44

Chapter 13: I Finish Everything I Start 47

Chapter 14: Foodbye 52

Chapter 15: Sir Paul, Heather, and the Standing Ovation 63

Chapter 16: Story Time with DAY (David A. Young) 70

Chapter 17: The Key to Your Heart 77

Chapter 18: Zarina, Zarina, Zarina 81

Chapter 19: And Still I Wait 84

Chapter 20: I'm Still Missing You 86

Chapter 21: More Soup — 92

Chapter 22: One-Woman Man — 96

Chapter 23: Gotta Get Close to You — 100

Chapter 24: Miscommunication — 103

Chapter 25: I've Given Up: I Can't Save You from You — 105

Chapter 26: Are You Following Me Around? — 122

Chapter 27: YouTube Link — 124

Chapter 28: 10/10/10 — 126

Chapter 29: Is He an Angel Now? — 131

Chapter 30: No Direction Calling Me Home — 136

Chapter 31: The Photograph — 138

Chapter 32: The Painting and the Rolling Stone — 145

Chapter 33: Layla — 158

Chapter 34: The Beatles and the Bard — 167

Chapter 35: 12/12/12 — 169

Chapter 36: Harrison House — 179

Chapter 37: Something in the Way She Moves — 182

Chapter 38: Just Be — 184

Chapter 39: Tom Petty and the Number 42 — 193

Chapter 40: Victoria and the Agent — 199

Chapter 41: Grandma Returns — 206

Chapter 42: Goodness — 211

Epilogue: St. George and the Dragon — 219

Appendix: In Memory of Mark Reale — 225

Acknowledgments — 231

About the Author — 235

Legend

by Doug Munson

A thousand years ago, according to English legend, a kingdom was threatened by a venomous dragon. The dragon would periodically demand a beautiful maiden as ransom. One day, the dragon claimed ransom of the king's daughter to spare the kingdom its wrath.

Upon hearing the princess was in peril of being consumed by the dragon, a gallant knight rushed to her aid on his white steed. A terrible battle ensued, but in the end, the good knight, whose name was George, slew the dragon in the soft tissue under its wing with lance and sword, sparing the kingdom and freeing the princess. Such is the legend of St. George and the dragon. Oh, and by the way, St. George is the patron saint of England.

Today, a thousand years later, this story lives on in metaphor for David Young. The venomous dragon is fear. Its hardened scales are doubts of all shapes and sizes. Our spiritual welfare is the kingdom at stake.

Chapter 1

1973

Picture, if you will, a fine day in 1973. Marina Ashley, a beautiful three-year-old maiden, plays in an English garden an hour outside the bustling city of London. The regal gardens and castle in the background stand like a giant mountain of affluence behind her, but she is unfettered by its enormity.

Three playful kittens jump in and out of Marina's arms and crawl across her shoulders. The music of her laughter fills the air and the hearts of those around her with its joyful innocence.

A man's soft voice with an English accent calls to her, "How do you like it so far?"

Marina tries to find the words to describe her bliss. "I love it, Uncle George. Can I stay here forever?"

"I hope you do, sweetheart," he answers.

George Harrison walks over to the elm tree where Marina's mom, Natasha, sits on the lawn reading her book in the afternoon sun. He massages her shoulders and gently kisses her ear.

"It's not as hot as Arizona, but it's not bad. I hope you enjoy it here."

Natasha lifts her head up, still deep in thought from what she was reading.

"Do you think we'll be able to find a yoga studio nearby? I loved the ashram." Looking over at her daughter she adds, "Marina certainly looks happy."

"I love her as my own. I want to give her everything she needs," he confesses. "The two of you bring me more joy than I've had in years."

A soft kiss, and Natasha continues reading her book.

▲ ▲ ▲

George met Natasha at the Sanskrit Ashram outside Tucson, Arizona the previous year.

They studied under Yogi Master Mahatma in the foothills of the Santa Catalina Mountain range. Natasha's relationship with Marina's father, Arnie, was ending. An enjoyable friendship had begun.

George was a fellow student, a new friend, and a former Beatle. They studied Hinduism, meditated, and practiced yoga together for months. Their friendship grew to the point where George did not want mother and daughter to stay behind when it came time to leave.

"I'm scheduled to record a new album and I have to return to England," he said. "How would you two like to come live with me?"

▲ ▲ ▲

Such is the story of why the beautiful young maiden and her mother were sitting together in George Harrison's English garden in the afternoon sun. The dragon was yet far away.

Chapter 2

October 2010

Let's skip ahead to October 2010. Marina is now a beautiful woman in her late thirties. Long brunette hair flows down past her shoulders as she sits with her five-year-old daughter Zarina in their Princeton home.

A white cat curls at Zarina's feet, purring softly. Marina glances at the unfinished painting hanging on the wall above the television set as they watch an afternoon children's show.

Zarina asks, "Mommy, when am I going to see Daddy again?"

"This weekend is his weekend with you, so it's just a few days away."

"Daddy said if I want to, I can learn an instrument when I'm older."

"What would you like to play?" Marina asks, as she braids Zarina's long blonde hair.

"I'm not sure. Something different. I don't like the piano. Too many notes."

"The guitar?"

"No, Mom, my friend has a guitar and it hurts my fingers."

"How about a flute?"

Zarina makes a questioning look as she turns her head.

Marina explains, "A flute sounds like a whistle, like . . . ." And she forms her lips to whistle a little tune for her.

"Maybe. But who is going to teach me?" Zarina asks, her big blue eyes looking up at her mother.

"I don't know. We'll have to find someone. Okay, time to get ready for dance class. Let's go."

They head out the door.

Chapter 3

This Change Is Gonna Do Me Good

Shortly before leaving my cherished home in suburban Minnesota, I heard the kitchen phone ringing. It was my former agent, David Krebs. He was just checking in to see how I was doing, so I told him. I think he got more than he bargained for.

"After the time, effort, and energy I put into the *Namasté* CD and all of the music videos," I blurted, "I can't afford to keep making vocal albums anymore. They don't sell for me. I'm only known for my instrumental music."

Silence.

"Listen, I'm never going to write another song again. I'm done. I can't afford to do projects like that anymore.

"Emma and I just split up after nine years, we're losing our house in a foreclosure, and I have to move back to the East Coast because I can't afford to be flying to these gigs across the country every weekend. Once I get to the East Coast, I'll just drive to my shows."

Silence.

"I don't care that the critics have been comparing my style to George Harrison. I'm sick and tired of writing songs that no one ever gets to hear."

The dragon rattled its scales in the distance.

The doorbell rang.

"I've got to go. This young guy I met at the editing facility asked me to help him finish a song and he just got here. Bye."

I hung up the phone and answered the door. Anish Das, a young, twenty-eight-year-old Indian waiter stands there.

"Hi, Anish. Come on in. Where's your guitar?"

"I didn't bring it," he responded.

"Then how are you going to show me the song?"

"I don't have a song to work on," he replied.

We sat down on the couch in the posh living room. I was puzzled as to why he was even there.

"Where's your lyric book?" (Something every songwriter has for his ideas.)

"I didn't bring it."

"I thought you had something started that I was going to help you finish."

"I just wanted to try writing with you. Jonathan played me some of your music videos and I really respect your writing." There was an uncomfortable pause.

"Well, thanks for the compliment, but if you don't have your lyric ideas or some chords to build from, what are we going to write about?"

"I don't know," Anish replied. Shaking my head, I pulled my acoustic guitar out of the case. I checked the tuning and played the opening chords to "This Change Is Gonna Do Me Good."

"Well, what do you think about this?"

"Sounds cool, I like it."

"Do you have an idea for some words?" I waited.

"No."

"How about a melody? Do you hear anything?"

I played a few more chords.

"No," he said shaking his head, embarrassed. I was getting a little flustered and couldn't believe that the guy came bringing nothing to the table and I really didn't want to write any more songs.

"What do you think about these words?" I asked.

People tell me every day, love is gonna come my way.
I'm searching for clues that I hope to find.

"Sounds cool," Anish answered blankly.

I continued with pen in hand, writing in my book, grumbling to myself as I wrote the rest of the words to the song.

I want a love that's gonna last,
I wanna live and forget the past.
I know this change is gonna do me good,
I know this change is gonna do me good.
I'm wondering where the wind will blow
If you've got a clue then let me know
Don't hold back now, give me a sign
Tell me something really good
Like, "live your dreams, you know you should"
I know this change is gonna do me good
I know this change is gonna do me good

Chapter 4

En Route to the Ashram

It wasn't long after that I pulled out of Minneapolis and headed east. My entire life was loaded into my car (clothes, boxes of CDs, musical instruments, and a cooler). It was a very emotional time, having just said goodbye to Wendy, Emma's daughter, who I'd grown to love deeply after nine years of being her stepfather. I was driving across the country to eventually move back to the East Coast. The economy was plummeting; the digital age had begun to kill CD sales. My 5,000-sq. ft. mansion was going into foreclosure, and I was alone in an SUV with whatever pieces were left of my life. My friends had all the confidence in the world that I would be fine, but I'd started my life from scratch before and knew all too well it's not an easy task.

As I was driving those seven hours to Chicago, I was literally hanging on by a thread, a thread that had been worn down to its last strand. At times, during the drive, I even considered driving the car into an oncoming truck, or off a bridge. Anything would have been better than the excruciating, devastating pain I was in. Instead, I decided to put on a CD, and pulled a handful of random disks out from the glove box. Speaking to God, I said aloud, "Pick me a good one." The lucky random CD was a Beatles album, *Sgt. Pepper's Lonely Hearts Club Band*. Since my heart was as lonely as a heart could be . . . *good choice*, I thought.

The George Harrison song, "Within You Without You," with sitars jangling and tablas pulsing, filled the car with mystical melody. George sang about how he and an imagined other spoke together about the love that lives inside us all.

My cell phone rang. "Hello Dave. It's Mike, Mike Marks from Brooklyn. How are ya?"

"Wow, Mike. I haven't heard from you in years, since high school in Brooklyn when I used to give you guitar lessons. How have you been?"

"I'm doin' okay, I guess. The economy sucks, but all in all, I guess I can't complain, ya know. What's all that loud music in the background? Are you in an Indian restaurant? It's hard to hear ya."

I turned down the car stereo.

"That's better. Where you at?" Mike continued.

"Well, I left Minneapolis a few hours ago; I'm heading to Chicago for a week to play at a yoga ashram and an art show after that. Then I'm headed back to New York."

"You moving back East?"

"Yeah, I guess so. Things didn't work out with Emma and it's so expensive to fly to shows now. I'm hoping that by living back east I can save money by just driving to my shows. I don't need to be making the airlines any richer."

"That makes sense. Well, when you get to New York you have to come see me. I started a new band on Long Island and you gotta come jam with us."

"Okay. Well, take care and I'll call you in a few weeks when I'm getting closer."

"See ya later."

I hung up and turned "Within You Without You" back up, blasting it in the car. When the song ended, I hit the Repeat button over and over for the next six hours until I arrived in Chicago at the ashram.

The Yogi Sadhan Ashram is located an hour southwest of Chicago in a beautiful wooded area. There is a large A-frame house filled with Hindu statues, Indian art, and artifacts.

Melanie, a good friend, greeted me with a warm caring hug. She had flown up from Florida to teach a yoga retreat at the ashram.

"How are you doing?" she asked.

"I'm doing okay. Could be better, I guess. I could be worse."

"Well, I didn't think you should have gone back to give it a second try after the last breakup you guys had."

"I know. I gave it my best shot."

"At least you have your music," Melanie added.

I unloaded my flutes from the car and handed a speaker to Melanie to carry. We entered the house where the first yoga session was about to take place, and Melanie introduced me to Hersh, the owner of the ashram. Hersh was a kind, middle-aged Indian woman with a peaceful aura. A host of other Indian ladies were preparing food in the kitchen.

"We have heard so much about your music and are so very honored to have you here," Hersh said in her thick accent. The other women joined in and agreed, bowing with hands at heart center, the traditional "Namasté."

"It's my pleasure to be here to play for you. What a peaceful place," I answered, looking around at all of the religious artwork. It was like a Hindu museum with paintings of Krishna and Arjuna driving a team of white horses on a chariot. Statues completely lined the windows. On the other side of the windows, a beautiful lawn stretched out about fifty yards from the main house.

"Let me show you to your room," Hersh said, motioning for me to follow her upstairs. "I think you will be very comfortable here this week. If you need anything, please let us know. Towels are here in this closet."

"Thank you. I'd like to lie down and rest for a bit. I'm a little tired after my seven-hour drive."

"The next session will be in one hour and we all look forward to hearing your music," she said, turning to leave. Then she closed the door behind her.

I dropped down on the bed with a long, deep sigh. Tears began to roll down my cheeks. I found myself whispering, "Starting my life over again," and I fell asleep.

▲ ▲ ▲

A gong woke me up. I went to my second-story window and, looking out, I could see towering oak trees. Thirty people assembled beneath them in yoga clothing with their yoga mats at the ready.

I grabbed my flutes and rushed downstairs to join them. I was just in time. Melanie was beginning to speak, hands together at her heart center. "My dear friends, today we are fortunate to have world-renowned musician and Grammy-nominated double flutist, David Young, perform sacred music for us during our yoga practice. David has been a close friend of mine for many years so please welcome him."

I saluted Namasté to them, bowing, brought my two flutes to my lips, and surrendered to the heavenly sound of the instruments I love. Melanie lead the group through the sun salutations, arms lifted up to the skies then hands flowing down in slow motion like angels in unison. For a moment, there is heaven on Earth here on this perfect summer day.

▲ ▲ ▲

After the yoga session was over, the group bowed Namasté in my direction, then to Melanie for teaching the class. Everyone was at peace, talking about how spiritual and beautiful the experience was.

An Indian man named Raj, deeply moved by the sacred music, approached me and spoke in a thick Indian accent. "Mister Young, you need to come with me to the Temple Thursday night. It would be such a blessing."

"Which temple's that?" I asked.

"The big Hindu Temple of Greater Chicago, of course. It is about half-an-hour from here. Will you come and play for us?"

"I don't know. I'm not sure if Melanie has something planned for me," I answered.

"Oh, you must come," he insisted. "It will be such a blessing."

I bowed Namasté to him and then politely walked away. He approached Melanie and discreetly asked, "Have you been to the Hindu temple?"

"No, I haven't, but I've heard a lot about it," she said.

After dinner, I retired to my bedroom. After a short meditation, I fell asleep. Suddenly I awoke in the dream world, walking with my guitar in a large room that resembled a trade show hall. Everything felt like it was moving in slow motion. At the end of the aisle was a drummer behind a drum kit, a bass player by his amp, and George Harrison standing there with a guitar slung over his shoulder. George was visibly upset. This was a shock to me.

I heard in my mind, as he was communicating to me without moving his lips: "You're late. We've been here waiting for you," George reprimanded me sternly. Embarrassed, I walked over to the empty space by my amplifier, lifted out my guitar, and started tuning up. There was serious tension in the room. The dream ended.

I woke up, not sure where I was, or why George Harrison was in my dream. The intensity still lingered. *At least that was just a dream*, I tried to reassure myself.

Chapter 5

The Flute and Krishna's Birthday

The following day, Raj approached me three times, each time with hands together at the heart center asking sincerely, "Are you coming to the temple?"

"I'm not sure," I replied. "We will see."

Thursday arrived and Raj did not show up for yoga until late afternoon. He hurriedly walked directly to me, breathing heavily. "I have come here today to bring you to the temple. It is very important."

I turned to Melanie and asked, "Is there anything planned for this evening?"

"No," she said.

"Do you want to come with me to this temple?" I asked her.

"I can't. The people who are putting me up have requested a private dinner with me." She added, "Why don't you go and you can tell me what it's like?"

"Okay, Raj. I guess I'll be going with you."

"You must bring your flutes," he reminded me.

The two of us drove for thirty minutes until the first sight of the temple perched up atop a hill. The temple grounds were the size of five football fields. Its white spires were so high they seemed to pierce the sky like majestic fingers. Peace and beauty emanated from this place. I felt like I was in a heavenly dream.

▲ ▲ ▲

We walked across the immaculate grounds, arriving at the main hall with ceilings thirty feet high. Large golden statuary was everywhere. Shoes were removed and everyone bowed to each other. The room was filled with hundreds of people dressed in colored saris. Many of the dark-complexioned women had gold rings in their noses.

Raj introduced me to the other musicians already at their instruments. A tabla player sat with his metallic Indian drum cradled between his crossed legs. Next to him was a man with a harmonium, a small wooden keyboard resembling an accordion. The right hand plays the twenty-four black and white keys while the left hand pumps a small handle.

Raj introduced the harmonium player first.

"David, this is Hitesh Master. He is the musical director of the temple."

After the customary bow, I said, "A pleasure to meet you. Did you say that your last name is Master?"

"Yes, my family members have been Master musicians in the King's court and royalty of India dating back 1,400 years. That is why my last name is Master."

The Hindu priest, dressed in a long flowing robe, walked in and the room fell silent. He approached me, tied a thin red piece of yarn around my right wrist, and bowed. I bowed back, and then he stepped up to his majestic golden chair on a small raised platform in the front. I sat with the band next to him.

As he began speaking in Hindi, the Indian woman next to me translated for me in a whisper.

"Today is a most special day, the holiday that honors one of our great saviors, Lord Krishna." After his short introduction, he motioned for Hitesh to start the music.

After a minute of playing and singing, Hitesh signaled me to start playing my flute along with them. The first song lasted thirty minutes. People threw money at me and danced around me as I sat on the floor and played.

The room erupted in joyous singing and whooping. Each new song we played was thirty to forty minutes long. The service lasted for over three hours.

Afterwards, each person in the room came over to me with the Namasté greeting. Raj beamed as he approached me. "Thank you so much for coming on this special day. Everyone loved you and said it was such a blessing having you here to play the flute."

"You're very welcome, Raj," I replied. "The energy here is incredible, so loving and beautiful. I don't know a great deal about Lord Krishna. What was he known for and why was it so important for me to be here tonight?"

Raj said, "Lord Krishna played the flute. Since we don't have a flute player, all the people felt it was a gift from the Gods that you were here to celebrate his birthday."

Chapter 6

I Sure Have Seen Better Days

I performed at the Chicago art festival over the weekend with renewed energy after the uplifting yoga retreat. Once the show was over, I hit the road again, continuing east to Ann Arbor, Michigan for another festival, then to Ashland, Ohio to visit my older brother, Howie.

Ashland is a small town about an hour and a half south of Cleveland. Howie's law practice is on Main Street and has been there for thirty years. He's been married to Lori, his college sweetheart, for at least that long. Howie's life path has been all about stability.

After a brotherly hug, Howie asked, "How you doing?"

"I'm okay," I responded solemnly.

We hung out in Howie's office until lunchtime. As we walked down the street to a coffee shop for something to eat, Howie looked at me squarely and said, "I don't know how you do it, Dave."

"What do you mean?" I asked, looking back at him.

"How do you deal with all of the changes that you've been through in your life? You must be made of Teflon," Howie commented, amazement in his eyes.

"Teflon?"

"Yeah. You can do almost anything to it and it still works. You've been through more moves, divorces, and struggles than anyone I know."

"Oh, this is getting old for sure. I think these changes were easier when I was younger."

"Where haven't you been?" Howie asked.

"Well, traveling forty weekends a year for eighteen years has taken me just about everywhere in America and quite a few places overseas. You remember, I lived in Los Angeles for ten years after Sarah, then Minneapolis for almost ten years with Emma . . . ."

"For a guy like me who has lived in the same house for more than twenty-five years, it's hard for me to keep up," Howie said.

"The thing that's made this even tougher has been saying goodbye to Wendy," I continued. "Since she lived with me all that time, she became like my own daughter."

"But she wasn't your biological daughter."

This hit a nerve with me. "Are you kidding me? Do you think that actually makes a difference? When you live with a kid, after a while it doesn't matter whether she was born with your genes or not. You love them like they are your own. I was never close with Mandy, Emma's younger daughter, but Wendy and I were tight."

"I didn't realize you were that close to her," Howie apologizes.

"When she was sixteen, she'd actually invite me out to the movies with her friends or her boyfriend. Did your son ever ask you to join him like that when he was a teenager?"

Howie made no comment. We arrived at Betsy's Sandwich Shop and I had to continue to drive my point home. "Anyone can be a parent, but it takes someone really special to be a step-parent. Very few people understand this and it's killing me. This is the second time I've had to say goodbye to a daughter. I haven't heard from my daughter AnnaLiise in years!"

Howie changed the subject as he opened the door and we walked into a country store with a lunch counter in the back. "Get whatever you want. The egg salad is good."

We walked to a table in the back. A TV monitor displayed a host chatting with their next guest, a famous spirit channeler.

Howie said, "This is such baloney. How can people believe in this junk?"

"Yeah, I don't get it either," I responded.

Howie tried to lighten up the vibe. "Well, I have a couple of things to tell you that you're gonna get a kick out of. First, I think you are finally famous."

"What makes you say that?" I was surprised to hear this from my businessman older brother, who's never been very interested in my career.

"I was in the Ashland library the other day. It's a small county library a few blocks from here. On the bottom shelf in the CD section, I saw one of your *Renaissance* CDs," he said smiling.

"Holy cow!" I responded sarcastically. "I have finally made it! You must be so proud."

"But that's not it." Howie smiled. "The best part of this story is still to come."

"Really? What a day. I'll have to write this down in my diary."

"One of my friends has a dog that has anxiety problems," Howie continued.

"I guess it's hard to find a good therapist around here," I quipped.

"So he took his dog to the vet and told the vet, 'Every time we leave the house, our dog goes into an emotional frenzy, and by the time they return, she's completely freaked out.'"

"Abandonment issues," I commented.

Howie ignored my remark and continued. "Apparently, lots of pet owners have this problem. So, get this, the doctor says, 'Get a copy of one of David Young's relaxing instrumental CDs and turn the music on when you leave the house. Your dog will relax and be at peace while everyone is away.' Can you believe it?" Howie laughed.

"Well, you gotta be famous for something," I quipped.

"So I told my friend to go down to the library and take out your *Renaissance* CD so he wouldn't have to purchase one."

"Thanks, Bro. Don't tell him to go to my website and buy one." I shook my head, taking the last bite of my sandwich and wiping my mouth with a napkin. "You know, when I was in rock bands, the worst thing you could say to someone is that their music put you to sleep. Now that's considered a compliment."

Howie got up and walked over to the register to pay the bill. He jokingly said to the waitress, "That's my brother

David, he's famous. His CD is in the library in the section where you can borrow CDs."

I rolled my eyes.

The waitress smiled at him and said, "I know who he is. I saw him interviewed on CNN a few years ago." She gave Howie back his change.

I thanked her kindly and we left the store.

When we got to my car, Howie stopped his joking. "Bro, hang in there. Let me know if you need anything."

"Thanks."

"You know what you have to do," he said. "You've got to put this all behind you and move forward."

"Yeah, I know."

After a long hug, I climbed back into my car and drove off. I put in a CD with a song I wrote called "I Sure Have Seen Better Days."

A storm is brewing
The seas are rising
And we're just waiting to watch it fall.
The left is swinging
While the right is righting
And nothing seems to make any sense at all.
And I've seen, yes I've seen
Oh, I sure have seen better days.
And I've seen, yes I've seen
Oh, I sure have seen better days

Chapter 7

The Concert for Bangladesh

I continued east through Pennsylvania and New Jersey towards New York. Throughout the drive, I unconsciously continued to hit the Repeat button on the CD player listening to "Within You Without You" over and over for hours each day.

I finally arrived in Glen Cove, New York, a suburb on the north shore of Long Island, to visit an old friend from school who found me on Facebook. Mike Marks was also good friends with my younger brother, so he was the only person from my childhood who knew that I'd changed my name to David Young. Still, I hadn't seen Mike for at least twenty-five years.

"Man, I can't believe how long it's been. It must have been high school when I played in a band with your brother Rob," Mike mused. "Come on in. Have a seat on the couch, here."

"You haven't changed a bit, David. You are forever young!"

"Yeah, that's my nickname, David Forever Young."

Mike continued. "My good buddy, Dave, I call him Big Dave, is the other guitar player in the band and he really wants to meet you. What do you think? Is it okay if we drive over there to say hi? He lives just fifteen minutes from here."

"Sure, why not."

After the short drive, we arrived at Big Dave's house and he greeted us at the door. Big Dave is a heavy-set guy with a big smile.

"David Young, so nice to meet you. Mike's told me all about you and I looked you up online. Way to go, man!"

We walked into the living room, which was full of guitars everywhere. A typical musician's home. Then I saw something that really piqued my interest on top of his TV—a DVD of *The Concert for Bangladesh*. I had to walk over and pick it up. "I've always wanted to see this. It must be thirty-five years old. Do you mind if we watch it now?" I asked. "I've been listening to a George Harrison song for days in my car."

Mike agreed, so we all watched the video together, talking about old times.

"I never knew much about George," I said.

Mike picked up a Les Paul guitar leaning against the couch and started playing it, unplugged. "Me neither. I was more into Zeppelin, Bad Company, and Montrose."

"Me, too. I could play every one of those songs note for note," I said.

"Yeah, me too."

"I wonder who taught you how to play all those tunes?" I said with a smirk.

Mike fessed up, "You were a great teacher, Dave."

"I had a great teacher, too. Mark from Riot never charged me a dollar. And he taught me everything."

"And then you taught me all the same stuff."

We focused on watching the concert video, and then it struck me. "George definitely had the vibe. Look at him. Everything he does is so Zen. I don't think any pop singer ever put as much spirituality into their songs as he did."

Mike shook his head and bent another note on the Les Paul. "I don't care about spirituality, I just wanna wail!"

I grew more contemplative, lost in the video, mesmerized.

When the video ended, Big Dave asked me, "Are you coming to the gig tonight?"

Mike added with excitement, "It's a big jam. Why don't you? You can play with us!"

"Well, as long as I'm back in New Jersey tomorrow morning. I have a show to do this weekend," I said.

"A rock show?" Big Dave asked.

"No, a flute show at an art festival. I never play guitar anymore. I make a living selling my instrumental CDs for yoga, relaxation, and meditation."

"Really?" Big Dave is perplexed. "Mike gave me a copy of your *Namasté* CD and I loved it! 'I Just Wanna Be Your Friend' is like one of the best songs of all time! It's so Bad Company."

"Thanks. What a nice compliment. Paul Rodgers was my favorite singer and people used to say that my voice sounded like his sometimes. I actually wrote that song as a take-off of a song by his early band Free, called, 'Baby Baby, Be My Friend.' Paul Kossoff, their lead guitarist, was one of my favorites because he had the best vibrato."

Later that night, we arrived at the club. Big Dave and Mike were playing the last set and the crowd was losing energy, as it was getting late.

They invited me up to play and I chose another Free song, "All Right Now." I sang and played the lead guitar and the place went crazy! They kept me up on stage and the bar owner kept the place open twenty minutes after closing because he didn't want me to stop.

The following morning, Mike's wife gave me a ride back to my mom's. Coincidentally, she worked five minutes from her apartment.

▲▲▲

I arrived at my mother's hi-rise apartment building in Cliffside Park, New Jersey, overlooking the Hudson River. After a loving hug and a sweet motherly kiss on the cheek, she asked, "So where are your adventures taking you next, my little traveler?"

Mom and I are close. I've shared most of my experiences on the road with her.

"I'm doing something I've never done before," I said.

"Oy, do I need to sit down?"

"No, this isn't anything too crazy. I'm just going to carpool with an artist friend down in Princeton and then we're driving together to Baltimore for the Sugarloaf Art Show. I can only stay a little while today. I need to take a cab for the ninety-mile ride south to Princeton."

I walked to the window, looking at the Hudson River with the Manhattan skyline hovering over it.

"So that's where it happened?" I asked.

"The miracle on the Hudson," she replied. "I was sitting here having my coffee about nine-thirty in the morning and the plane landed right down there," pointing down to the river. "You have to believe in miracles. When your life is about to crash, you have to have faith that something is going to be there to catch you so you don't drown."

"I hope so."

All too soon, the car service arrived and whisked me off to Princeton. I have to admit, it felt nice to not have to drive for a change, but I missed George's song. When I arrived in Princeton, my artist friend, John, greeted me. John's been doing the art festival circuit for years and is known for his drawings of John Lennon. We loaded my sound system, clothes bag, flutes, and CDs into the side of his white van, and off we went.

"Thanks for letting me ride with you down to the show. I'm tired of driving," I said as I jumped into the passenger seat.

Sitting on the dashboard of the van was a cassette tape of *The Concert for Bangladesh*!

"What is this doing here?" I exclaimed in amazement. I was freaked out.

"I just pulled it out of a box that was in my attic for the past thirty-nine years to listen to on the drive. It was a great concert."

"You were there?"

"Yes, I was," John said proudly. "I paid $3.50 each for two tickets! I still have the stubs."

I picked up the old cassette tape of *The Concert for Bangladesh* with the picture of the starving boy on its cover, marveling at the days' coincidence. "Wow . . . I just watched this at a friend's house yesterday. I can't believe this is here again in your van!"

And we were on our way.

Chapter 8

The Online Dating Adventures

After two months of living in New Jersey, I'd had enough. Trying to start a new life in this unfriendly big city was not working for me. I reconnected with some old friends I knew from Eckankar, a spiritual group where I learned meditation years ago, and decided to move down to the Philadelphia area. Most of them were married and there were no eligible single women in our circle.

Since I didn't care for the bar scene anymore, I logged onto a singles website to try to meet someone. I had two dates through the site and each one was worse than the other. Both women were at least ten years older and ten pounds heavier in real life than they were in their profile pictures. That was enough for me to give up online dating.

But a third woman viewed my profile and contacted me, which was a first.

Could it be something good is finally happening? I asked myself. Her name was Theresa and she had grown up close to where I was living, near Princeton. She contacted me because she was planning on moving back to the area.

She lived in Scranton, Pennsylvania. Since I was new to the area, I wasn't aware of how far away Scranton was from Newtown, where I shared a house with another Eckankar member named Karen.

As I got to know Theresa through email, she appeared to be spiritual. She enjoyed writing poetry, which was cool. And her poems were really well-done.

After a little research, I discovered that Scranton was two-and-a-half hours away! Normally, I would not have driven that far to go on a date. But I really enjoyed our conversations, and her pictures . . . so I decided to drive up the following day and planned to also visit an old friend in the music business.

Carl Canedy, a rock producer/drummer I knew from twenty-five years ago, lived in Scranton. Back in his rock'n'roll days, Carl produced the band Anthrax, whose singer Joey Belladonna played in a band with me in college. I reconnected with him and explained how I met a woman on an online dating site who lived in the vicinity, so I was planning to come up to visit.

"Hey, if it works out with her, maybe we could start recording a project together before she moves down closer to Philly," I suggested. Although Carl was a world-class drummer and producer, he couldn't find many musicians in Scranton to play with.

The following day, I decided to make the two-and-a-half-hour drive up to take her out. I was to meet Theresa at the Olive Garden at 12:30 p.m. I arranged a meeting with Carl for 3:00 p.m., and planned on taking Theresa out to dinner too.

A vicious, windy rain pelted me during the entire drive. It was so windy it almost blew my car off the road while driving over one of the mountain roads. It took three hours to get there. I arrived at the restaurant and asked for a quiet, romantic table. Theresa texted that she'd be fifteen minutes late. I waited outside the restaurant under an awning as the rain continued to pour.

Finally, a woman who looked kind of like her profile picture got out of her car, and walked toward me in slow motion. The closer she got, I could see that she didn't look like her pictures. As she approached the front door, I said, "Theresa?" but she ignored me, opened the front door and entered the restaurant. "Thank God it wasn't her!" I said, and let out a long, deep sigh.

Soon after, Theresa drove by in her sporty silver Mustang. She looked cute in the distance, and waved to me while looking for a parking space. Since it was raining hard, I walked out to the parking lot and over to her car with my umbrella so she wouldn't get wet. Our eyes met, and when she stepped out of the car I knew in an instant that it wasn't going to happen.

Carl was the first person I saw at another restaurant after the lunch. I told him I wouldn't be coming back to Scranton to see Theresa. So we diverted the conversation to catching up.

"I remember when I saw you playing at Universal Citywalk in 1991, when you were first getting started with

Celestial Winds. There was a huge crowd buying your tapes, and it was so incredible to see."

"Oh, I was just trying to make a living. My vocal music never made me any money and for some reason people really wanted to buy my flute music."

Carl continued, "You started the whole 'Do-It-Yourself' way of selling music that is the standard now with bands. You were ahead of your time!"

"I never thought it would turn into anything. I was just down to my last hundred dollars when I started. Then I sold a million CDs, and things were going great. But it didn't last forever. Everything is so much more difficult now. I'm lucky I'm able to do art shows and conventions all over the country and still make a living. But I'm sorry, I guess I won't be coming back up here to record that project with you."

Carl laughed, "I guess not!"

Chapter 9

Yogaphoria

I pulled back onto the highway after lunch with Carl and began the long drive back to Newtown when my cell phone rang. It was my friend Lisa who lives in Yardley, the next town over from Newtown. She was calling to see how the date went. I told her the whole story.

Lisa said, "Well, I have some good news for you. While I was at the gym today, I saw my friend Monica and told her all about you. She went to your website and said she'd like to meet you. She has blonde hair and blue eyes. She's petite and a cutie. So cheer up!"

"Wow, that was so kind of you. Thanks, I really needed something good to happen after this day," I said.

Lisa gave me her phone number. "Call me when you get back into town later."

I called Monica and had a really nice chat with her on the way home. We made plans to have coffee in a few days' time.

Word got around to my new friends about the date up in Scranton. Gregg, a singer, songwriter, and acoustic guitarist who I'd met at a party, met me for lunch.

"How's the dating scene going?" Gregg asked.

"Not good." I gave him a rundown of my online dating episodes. "I am done with Internet dating forever."

When Gregg finally stopped laughing, he said, "I have some good news for you. I told my girlfriend about you and she wants to introduce you to her best friend."

"What is she like?"

"You won't be disappointed, believe me. She used to be an actress and model. She owns a yoga studio."

"I love yoga. She must be spiritual. What else?" I perked up.

"You guys also have something else in common."

"What's that?"

"*Seinfeld*. She was the actress on the famous 'shrinkage' episode, and you inspired the 'puffy shirt' episode. She also lived in Los Angeles. I think you're going to like her. She has the coolest studio in New Hope called Yogaphoria." Gregg gave me her phone number. "Give her a call, her name is Stephanie."

A few days later, I visited Yogaphoria for a yoga class and introduced myself. "Gregg said we have a few things in common. Would you be interested in lunch?"

There was a pleasant vibe and nice attraction between us. She was as beautiful as Gregg described, with long dark flowing hair, brown eyes, and a voluptuous yoga body. After a few dates, I offered to perform for her yoga class and she accepted my offer. Posters were created and emails were sent out to publicize the event set for Saturday, October 9th, a few weeks away. I took the weekend off to help her out.

During this time, I also enjoyed nice phone conversations with Monica, Lisa's friend. We set a date to get together, but then she had to postpone because her office was being moved to another location. So we made new plans for Sunday, October 10th—the day after the yoga performance.

On October 9th, I arrived at Yogaphoria early to set up for the event that was to start at 10:30 a.m. Stephanie welcomed me and showed me in.

"Would you like to spend the rest of the day with me after the session is over?" I asked.

"That would be nice, but I just got back together with my old boyfriend and I'm leaving for the weekend after the event," she said.

That was not the answer I expected.

Later that afternoon, Monica called. She was sniffling and her voice sounded nasal. "I think I'm getting the flu. I'll call you Sunday morning to let you know whether the medicine I took got rid of what I have or if I'm too sick for our date. I'm really sorry."

When she called back Sunday morning, her voice sounded worse. She was definitely too sick to get out of bed. Now, on my rare weekend off, I suddenly had no plans.

Chapter 10

One Look

Amutual friend had introduced me to a guy named Kartikeya who played tabla and Indian drums. I gave him a call. During the course of our conversation, I said, "I'm always working on the weekends and to have a day off with nothing to do is a bummer. Do you know of anything going on today?"

Kartikeya responded, "Some friends are going to meet over in Hopewell, New Jersey to play touch football. If you would like to come play, that would be fine."

"Where's Hopewell?"

"It's about a half-hour from where you live in Newtown."

"Okay, give me directions and I'll see you there."

I drove to the football field expecting to see a bunch of guys, but when I arrived Kartikeya was chatting with a woman sitting on the grass. She was an attractive brunette wearing a baseball cap and a loose football shirt. Definitely not the bunch of guys I expected to be playing with. Her name was Marina.

"Where is the rest of the team?" I asked.

"More people are coming," said Kartikeya.

"Is she playing with us, too?" I asked. I'd never played sports with a woman before.

"Yeah, she's playing, and she's good!" Kartikeya replies.

I sat down with two of them, introduced myself, and explained to Marina who I am and what I do. A half-hour later, a few other guys showed up. Only when she stood up to start playing did I realize her height. She was a little taller than I am. After tossing the ball around, we broke into teams and started to play. Marina was on my team. Kartikeya was right. She was good.

One look was all it took and I was sold on you
One kiss could make me rich, make me well-to-do
So fine if you were mine and I was yours too
Someday, listen when I say, I'm gonna be with you
I've been lonely, you've been lonely too
I've been lonely, wanna give all my love to you

Chapter 11

Come Home with Me

Another guy arrived on the scene. Marina ran over to give him a hug, then got back in the game. There was a lot of running around, laughing, and chasing each other. We strategized in the huddle. With our backs to the other team, we sketched out the plays on her stomach—a bit awkward, as her breasts kept getting in the way. I decided it would be better to diagram the plays on my own chest.

We bonded and had great fun playing. Some of the other guys had to go, leaving Marina and me on a team by ourselves. While short of breath from running, I asked Marina in the next huddle, "I have two questions. One . . . Is that your boyfriend?"

"No."

"Good. Two . . . Are you in love with anyone?"

"Not really."

"Okay, the next play is . . . ."

We made a good team. She could run and catch the ball better than any female I'd ever seen. I was the quarterback on most of the plays. She was the receiver.

After the game, she said she had to leave and get ready for her yoga.

"Really? I love yoga," I said. "I did a yoga class this morning."

"I'm a yoga instructor."

This just keeps getting better, I thought to myself.

"I'd love to join you," I said.

"Kartikeya can tell you where it is. I'll see you at seven," Marina said, and ran off the field.

"How can a woman that beautiful not have a boyfriend?" I asked Kartikeya.

"How do you know she doesn't have a boyfriend?"

I just thought to myself, *The way she looked at me and the fun we had . . . there's no way she has a boyfriend now.*

Just before seven that night, I arrived at Marina's yoga studio. I paid for the class and went into the spacious room. I gazed at the hardwood floors and yoga posters on the walls. Then she entered the room, dressed in a white skintight outfit embellished with an Asian dragon design. *Whoa . . .* the dragon. The loose-fitting jersey she wore while we played football earlier completely hid her incredible body.

I handed her one of my yoga CDs, *Creation*, to play in the class.

"I don't ever play music in my class that I haven't listened to first," Marina said.

"I completely understand."

After a moment, I said, "Marie Diamond, the world-renowned Feng Shui master who was in the movie *The Secret*, said she had the most profound spiritual experience of her life while I performed one of the songs from this in concert."

She paused and looked down at the cover, illustrating a spiritual light at the end of a blue tunnel.

"I think it would be okay to play this one."

I have to admit, the music did create a beautiful spiritual ambiance in the room. Her yoga attire accentuated her perfect body as she moved fluidly through the different asanas with the class. I tried desperately not to be distracted by how sexy she was and stay focused, but I did peek once in a while, thinking, *Oh, my God, this is getting better every minute.*

Suddenly, she moved through a series of amazing asanas that I'd never seen before. I wouldn't have believed they were possible. It appeared as if she was levitating. I struggled to keep up, but kept smiling from ear to ear.

The class ended and she announced, "That wonderful music we just heard was David's music," and introduced me. A few people asked where they could buy copies of it. Then, one by one everyone left.

I waited for Marina by the front door, and when she arrived I asked, "Do you want to get something to eat?"

"Sure, but I have to give someone a ride home first."

I wondered what that was all about. *Is this a guy she's dating or an ex-boyfriend or a husband?* I thought. I followed her in my car back into town. Marina dropped off her passenger, parked her car in her garage, and jumped into my sports car.

"Who was that?" I asked, almost afraid of the answer.

"He's my next-door neighbor. His wife let him out to do yoga with us," she answered.

I hid my sigh of relief.

We drove to a restaurant close by called the Blue Moon Café, and each ordered a light salad with some herbal tea.

I opened the conversation. "That was a nice class. I really enjoyed it."

"Thanks, David. I could see that you've been doing yoga for a while."

"About three years. It's a great de-stressor. I actually did another class this morning before football," I added, just for good measure.

"Two yoga classes in one day. Impressive."

I took the initiative, "So, tell me about you. What else do you do besides yoga and playing football better than any woman I've ever met?"

Marina smiled, "I'm the mom of a five-year-old little girl named Zarina. She's the love of my life. And I am an actress, model, and a company spokesperson."

"And Zarina's dad, do you guys get along?" I ask.

"It's amicable."

"How come you're not still together?"

"Let's just say that he didn't keep up his end of the bargain."

Since the cafe was close to where we played football that afternoon, we walked back to the field after eating, talking, and getting to know each other.

It's been nice talking to you
I see we have so much in common

We've both seen a lot of life
and we've both been down to the bottom
You look troubled I can see, as confused as me
But no one as cute as you should be this lonely
I'm so tired of being alone,
you're so tired of being alone
But no one as cute as you should be this lonely
Why don't you come home with me.
Come home with me
Well you just lost the love of your life,
congratulations I just lost mine
And you're wondering where the years disappeared
And got lost in the passage of time
I'm so tired of being alone,
you're so tired of being alone
But no one as cute as you should be this lonely
Why don't you come home with me.
Come home with me
Everyone needs someone to love,
everyone deserves one last try
This could be our last chance to find true love
And turn our sorry story into a lullaby
Why don't you come home with me . . . .

▲ ▲ ▲

We found a place to sit in a quaint, white gazebo in the moonlight.

"What brings you to the area?" she asked.

"I ended a nine-year relationship about five months ago. I was the step-dad to my ex's two daughters. I needed to make a new start and I have a few friends who live in the Yardley area."

"Are you still in touch with the girls?" she asked.

"I was very close to the older one, Wendy, and we text each other all the time. The younger one and I never really connected."

"That's so nice that you keep in touch with her."

"After living with a child for nine years, you don't stop caring about them just because you weren't there when they were born. People don't realize how close step-dads get to the kids."

Marina was silent.

"I had a foster child. She was fifteen and lived with us for four months. When she left, it broke my heart; that was painful."

"Then you can kind of understand how I feel," I said. "Life has so many disappointments."

"You're not the only one with disappointments, either," she pointed out.

After about a half-hour of chatting by the gazebo, I asked her, "Can I kiss you?"

"Isn't that a little quick?"

That was not the answer I expected. It didn't seem quick to me after feeling so connected the whole day. But I replied, "I guess so . . . ."

Changing the subject, I said, "It's getting chilly. Like to go for a ride before I take you back home?"

"Sure."

Chapter 12

Whatever Road You Choose

It was about 10:00 p.m., so we took a drive through the country. The top was down, letting a nice breeze blow through our hair like a relaxing massage.

I asked, "Would you like to hear some of my vocal music?"

"Okay."

I turned on the *Namasté* CD. "Want to hear me sing along?"

"No, you don't have to do that," she answered diplomatically.

After she heard track nine, "Whatever Road You Choose," she said, "Play that again, I love that one!"

You're heading down this road, I see a change coming
There's tears in your eyes, decisions must be made
There's times in your life you just feel like running
Whatever you do, whatever you do
Whatever road you choose, I'm gonna be there for you
Whatever you decide, I'm gonna be by your side

Whatever road you choose, I'm gonna be there for you
Whatever you do, I'm gonna be here for you

It's hard for me to see this crossroad you're on
And it's hard when I know mistakes have been made
There's times in your life you just feel like crying
There's cards on the table and one must be played
Whatever you do, whatever you do
Whatever road you choose, I'm gonna be there for you
Whatever you decide, I'm gonna be by your side
Whatever road you choose, I'm gonna be there for you
Whatever you do, I'm gonna be here for you
Roadblocks and detours, wrestling with doubt
This life is a journey worth figuring out
Wherever you are, wherever you are
Whatever road you choose, I'm gonna be there for you

▲ ▲ ▲

After hearing it the second time, Marina said, "That one is definitely my favorite. Why did you write it?"

I explained, "Even though it sounds like it could be about a woman, it's actually about a conversation I was having with God. I'd just finished this album and I was meditating about what was going to happen with it. I've been lucky to have success with my instrumental music, but my vocal music hasn't had great success. It's weird, though, whenever I've been to a psychic, they always tell me that my words are healing and that's what I should really be doing.

"So I asked God if I should put more energy into my vocal music. This was the answer that came to me, 'Whatever road you choose, I'll be there for you. Whatever you decide, I'll be by your side. Whatever road you choose, I'll be there for you.'"

"Wow." That's all Marina said. But the way she said it, I could see that she got it.

My first swipe at her dragon of fear and doubt.

By that time, we'd arrived at her house.

"It was great spending the day with you," she said.

"It definitely was. Here, you can have the CD since you loved that song so much."

"Thanks, I will surely listen to it."

"Nice meeting you," I said, and gave her my best smile.

"Bye, David."

I did not try to kiss her, much as it pained me. She just got out of the car and walked into her house. I just drove off.

When I arrived back home after the half-hour drive, I noticed a text message on my cell. It was from Marina, "If I never see you again, I LOVE that today happened."

I texted back, "Me, too."

Maybe the dragon was going away.

Chapter 13

I Finish Everything I Start

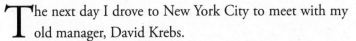

The next day I drove to New York City to meet with my old manager, David Krebs.

I texted Marina in the morning, telling her I'd be passing through New Jersey close to where she lived on my way back. Maybe I could stop by. We could have dinner and I could meet her daughter. She said that sounded like a great idea. During the day, she texted me twice to see how my day was going. I took it as a good sign that she took the initiative to communicate with me. Could it be she likes me? She texted how much she loved the song, "Whatever Road You Choose" on the *Namasté* CD and said she played it over and over all day long.

I arrived at her house about 6:30. Marina welcomed me in. An unfinished painting above the television caught my eye.

"This painting is beautiful. I love the colors. Why isn't the right side finished?" I asked.

"Oh, I just never got around to it."

Hmm, I finish everything I start, I thought to myself.

Marina was dressed in a hippie skirt and wore no makeup. She looked relaxed, but didn't have the pizzazz of the previous night without her makeup. I'm afraid she sensed that I didn't seem wowed by her. Her daughter Zarina was on the front porch of their house. She had long, wavy blonde hair and fair skin. We decided that, since it was such a beautiful evening and autumn was coming, we should go out for a walk in the woods. Marina went back inside the house. Zarina and I continued chatting and getting to know each other.

When Marina came out ten minutes later, she had makeup on again. I interpreted this as a sign she wanted to look her best for me. Zarina and two of her little friends joined us. Zarina reminded me of Mandy, Emma's younger daughter, except Zarina smiled at me as we got to know each other. The resemblance between Zarina and Mandy was uncanny. When Zarina smiled at me, it was like healing salve on an old wound. Mandy had rejected me for nine years. No matter how much I tried, or how much love I offered her, she kept her distance. Zarina, on the other hand, welcomed the new friendship.

Marina gathered up Zarina and the two neighbor girlfriends from down the street, loaded them into her car, and we drove to a park to go for a walk in the woods. As we walked, I hoisted Zarina up on my shoulders, just like I did with Mandy when she was that age. It was starting to feel like I'd found a new family, even though it was only our second day together. I knew from previous experience that when you meet a woman who has kids, the relationship with the kids is every bit as important as with their mother. I was enjoying Zarina very much and everything was falling into place.

Marina explained a little about her childhood.

"I grew up in Colorado, and my mom was into Hinduism."

"Any brothers? Sisters?" I asked.

"I was an only child."

"And your father?"

"My dad passed away when I was younger, and my mom's been ill lately. Sometimes this is very difficult. Recently, I've had terrible insomnia and I've been up too many nights without good rest."

I took Zarina down from my shoulders and she ran ahead to her friends.

"Relationships?" I asked.

"I've been extremely disappointed by men recently. Because of that, I am in no way ready to start a relationship anytime soon."

The dragon was back!

▲ ▲ ▲

Marina seemed to enjoy my company, even welcome it. I thought maybe I could help her heal. I was thinking, *I'm a nice guy and maybe my good vibes will carry over to her.*

We arrived back at her house after the walk and she whipped up an incredible soup with barley and a variety of vegetables grown in her backyard. She was a big-time vegetarian. The soup was amazing. I complimented her on it repeatedly. She offered to give me some to go. I gladly accepted.

Just before leaving, I said, "I'm flying to Arkansas tomorrow to do an art show from Wednesday to Sunday, and will return late Sunday night. There are lots of vendors selling everything from jewelry to Christmas items, and I play on and off throughout the day."

Marina told me to keep in touch while I was away. I did not try to kiss her goodbye.

The next day we texted each other about how nice it had been spending time together.

Marina wrote, "Stay in touch. I'm looking forward to your return."

Thinking I was being funny, I wrote, "I hope our conversations weren't too deep for you."

Marina texted back, "You're not the only person with depth around here! Goodbye, David."

The dragon roared so loud it must've sent Mercury into retrograde. Her comment sounded like she was insulted. I tried calling her to resolve this, but she didn't answer. I texted her to explain that I was just kidding. She didn't answer back. An hour went by without hearing back from her. The dragon struck and just ended our friendship.

Parking was on the other side of the airport, and I had a long walk to get back to the terminal. Consequently, I missed my flight and the airline charged me $150 to put me on the next flight. They also charged me another $150 for my three bags. The day had turned into a disaster. Another victory for the dragon.

As the plane was boarding ninety minutes later, Marina finally texted me back. "Oh, no, you misunderstood me. My phone was turned off because I was in a photo shoot. Have a safe flight." I got on the plane to fly to Arkansas, worn out but grateful that the dragon backed off and that my new relationship with Marina was not over.

It's the change of a season,
The fall leaves are leaving
This year is fading away
And as I look back and relive my tracks
I look forward to brighter days
And tomorrow's a moment away
Tomorrow's a moment away
Yesterday's gone, yesterday's gone, yesterday's gone away
Yesterday's gone, yesterday's gone, yesterday's gone away
All of these changes, changes
Life keeps on changing, changing
I guess I'll keep changing

Chapter 14

Foodbye

I arrived in Arkansas for the outdoor festival, and the texting continued with Marina.

She wrote, "I just found out that the day we met, 10/10/10, was a magical day astrologically. There's so much chatter about it on the Internet now. It means incredibly good things."

"Wow, that's cool," I wrote back. "What are people saying?"

"It's supposed to mark a whole new beginning of spirituality manifesting on Earth."

We were in constant contact via text the following days. Marina shared that white and cream were her two favorite colors. This was odd because I've been known for wearing white and cream. Some of my friends actually have gone to my closet just to look at all of my white and cream clothes lined up one after the other.

Marina texted, "Did we really just meet a week ago? I can't wait for you to come back." A very positive sign. *Ah, goodbye dragon . . . .*

During breaks at the show, I walked around chatting with other vendors. It's customary for artists to trade or give discounts to each other. I found a white sweater, a colorful blouse, matching necklace, earrings and ankle bracelet, plus some herbal teas for good measure.

Marina texted, "I am now in love with your music."

"I'm really glad you're enjoying it," I wrote back.

Marina continued, "I can't play anything in my house except your music now. It's like your music is the soundtrack in my life!"

"Thank you! Do you have a favorite?" I asked.

"Definitely number nine. Do you think I can send one of these and one of your yoga CDs to my mother in New Mexico? I think she'll love *Namasté* because of the meaning behind the lyrics. She's a real New Ager."

"Of course." I interpreted this to mean she wanted her mom to check out the new man in her life. Another good sign.

Marina started asking about my relationship with Emma. "Do you plan on ever going back to Minneapolis?"

"No way," I replied.

"Are you sure it is over?"

"I'm done! I gave it my best shot and there's no point."

I wondered, *Does this mean she wants to be sure I'm unattached before she really gets involved emotionally?* All of our communication seemed to be in harmony.

Taking these questions into account, I started allowing the feelings I had for her to grow—in spite of the fact that she said a week before that she was not in a place to start a relationship. While at the fair, I began writing these lyrics:

You're a woman of integrity; I'm a man of integrity
You're a woman of sincerity, and I'm a man with this quality
The more of you that I see,
the more I believe this is destined to be

I counted the days until I would return. Apparently, her insomnia was contagious because now I was up restless every night at 3:00 a.m. The only thing I could think of to pass the time was to serenade myself with my guitar while lying in my hotel room. There is one piece of music that I played over and over. This was my favorite piece, though I'd never written lyrics for it. Each time I picked up a guitar this would be the first thing I'd play. The words I wrote at the festival fit perfectly to it. Over the following weeks, the rest of the lyrics were rewritten six times. And I had never done that.

During my sleepless hours, I became obsessed with this song. I thought that when she heard its sincerity and beauty, Marina would finally believe that I was sincere. Maybe she would trust me enough to let her guard down and let me into her heart. Hour after hour, I played this song during the night, putting myself into a trance with it.

During the show the next day, I texted her, "I've written a song for you that I think is ridiculously beautiful."

"When am I going to hear it?" she asked.

"I don't know," I answered.

Sunday, the last day of the show, finally arrived.

Marina texted, "I'm really looking forward to you coming home."

I felt the same way. My flight had one stopover in Houston, and would arrive at 1:00 a.m. I found out there was a direct flight arriving at 10:00 p.m. and decided to drive to the airport to try to change it. The airline personnel were incredibly nice and made the change for me, no charge. They upgraded my ticket to first class and waived the baggage fees as well. All the negative energy from the original flight down was now turned around.

I texted Marina with the good news. "I'm taking an earlier flight so I can come see you on my way home from the airport . . . at about 10:30 p.m."

"Great!" she responded.

I took the rest of the afternoon off from playing at the festival, and just sat in a park daydreaming. It looked like my life was finally on track.

Marina texted, "The universe is rewarding you for getting through the horrible day of flying to Arkansas, and now everything is going to be perfect for you."

I boarded the flight, feeling like a rock star. After settling in, I began a peaceful meditation that lasted for ninety minutes. This was something I'd rarely done for that long a stretch. I experienced an unusually deep spiritual state of inner peace.

The flight arrived a half-hour early at Newark Airport. I texted Marina, "I will be getting there earlier than expected, around 10:00 p.m."

No response.

I picked up my luggage and was on my way to the airport shuttle to get my car when her text arrived. "My insomnia has been terrible, and I have not slept in days. I have to go to sleep. I am exhausted. I'll see you in a couple of days."

What? I tried calling her, but she didn't pick up. Confused, I left this message, "I have been so looking forward to seeing you all week. I took this earlier flight home and missed part of my show so I could see you tonight. Is it okay if I just stop by for fifteen minutes on my way home?"

She didn't respond. I sent the same message again.

Finally Marina texted back, "That would be too dangerous."

I was confused and texted, "I bought some gifts for you at my show and I'm excited to give them to you."

Marina didn't respond.

I hate these head games; they're the last thing I want! I contemplated what to do next while driving on the winding roads of the New Jersey Turnpike. I decided to send this frustrated message. "I'm just going to leave these gifts on your porch, so make sure you bring them in. There are valuable things in there. Foodbye." (I hit the wrong key by mistake.)

I drove to her house and left the box with the jewelry, blouse, and the sweater by her front door.

The dragon hit me with a fiery blow.

▲ ▲ ▲

Disappointed, pissed off, confused, and disillusioned, I returned home and turned on my laptop, trying to calm down.

Though I wanted to write an angry letter to her, I decided to try to write a gentle one.

Subject: I would love to understand . . . .
Date: Mon, 18 Oct 2010 00:01:02 -0500

Marina,

I wish you could feel comfortable enough to be honest with me.

A lot of this does not make sense.

Please help me understand you.

And a phone call or a meeting would be so much better . . . .

   Sincerely,
David

The following morning I received this response.

From: Marina
Subject: I hope this helps (a little)
Date: Mon, 18 Oct 2010 07:48:44 -0400

Good morning—

I feel really badly about last night . . . and thank you so kindly for the gifts . . . that was really so thoughtful (and totally unnecessary) . . . but I could tell your heart was in it.

I'm not really sure what to say as I feel like we're in different places and I also feel like you read into things possibly more than me . . . I do care about you, from what I know . . . but I also see you as very fragile, and in a way, I'm not sure whether you're interested in me or just finding love—filling a void (not that there's anything wrong with that).

Because of my insomnia, I suppose, I become really "out of it" at night . . . and therefore, don't like talking on the phone . . . at all. I realize that texting is no substitute for in-person or a real conversation, but at night, I'm usually catching up with friends and I have a few conversations, via text, going on. Again, not that this is the right way—but it seems to work best for me. It's difficult for me to have much of a conversation in the day (because of Zarina) and at night, it doesn't work well for me. So, it's nothing against you.

I have to confess, your sensitivity and abruptness makes me uncomfortable. Just the way you interpreted one of my texts before you left . . . and now. Did I mislead you? If so, that was not my intention. I was enjoying the moment and sensed that you were also, but you were jumping ahead.

I thought I was clear that I am in a strange place right now (with regard to love) . . . and I'm just not eager to let anyone 'in' anytime soon.

We can talk more (over the phone), but for now, I just wanted to address these few things.

In peace,
Marina

From: David
To: Marina
Subject: I hope this helps (a little) . . . thanks.
Date: Mon, 18 Oct 2010 09:43:08 -0500

Good morning.

Thanks for your email. It helped me to understand some things about your communicating. They say that 50% of all texts/emails are misunderstood and so if only 1% of ours has been misunderstood, I think we are doing pretty well.

You were clear that you were in a strange place when I first met you. But it's hard to deny the wonderful things that have happened between us. We have a nice natural vibe and, in my opinion, I think we could be helpful to each other emotionally because I think our natural qualities are the qualities that our former partners lacked. I think that's an important reason for the universe to bring two people together, among others. I think the universe wants us to believe in Love and find true lasting happiness with someone. And I believe that you are developing feelings for me, even though there's a part of you that doesn't want to let yourself have feelings for anyone. I think what each of us could really use right now from the opposite gender is what each of us has to offer.

Who hasn't been let down by their partner's shortsighted decisions? The opposite of that is sincerity, and that's one of my strongest qualities.

Sincerity over time would be a cure for someone who has been let down. I wrote about this in the ridiculously beautiful song I wrote for you.

I don't think you realize how wonderful you are, and how nice it is to be around you. I don't think you give yourself enough credit in that regard.

Life is giving me this great opportunity to learn and practice patience with you, and I can definitely use practice in that. Life is giving you the opportunity to see that there is a special person who has come into your life that you could actually be able to believe in and trust.

We can talk when you have time.

Namasté, truly meant,
David

▲▲▲

Marina and I talked in the morning, and planned to meet a few days later at a coffee shop near her house. I arrived about twenty minutes early and decided to go to the field where we played football, since I had the extra time.

I walked to the spot where we first met on the grass. I crouched down and said a little prayer. "If it is meant to be for Marina and me to resolve this, then let it be. And if not, then it is in YOUR hands."

I kissed the palm of my hand, placed it on the ground where she had been sitting that first day, then drove back to the coffee shop to wait for her.

When Marina arrived she was cordial, but not as open as she had been the previous week. She wore the blouse I bought at the show. She ordered a latte. I ordered a bowl of soup.

It's not half as good as her soup, I thought. When the waitress brought my change, it included a one-dollar bill with the words "Where's George.com?" written on it in blue ink.

After some small talk, Marina spoke her mind.

"I talked with a couple of friends who said they thought you were nuts for ending our friendship and texting me FOODBYE.

"Then, leaving those gifts on my porch because I was too tired to get together. My friends said I should run the other way and never talk to you again."

I thought to myself, *If you really didn't care about me, why didn't you just stop returning my calls and forget about me? Why would you even take the time to ask your friends?*

I took a second to respond. "Well, I spoke with two of my friends, to make sure I wasn't off track and misreading you and they thought the same things I did."

"What do you mean?" she asked.

"You said you wanted to send my CDs to your mom. My friends also interpreted that as you wanting your mom to check out the new man in your life. And when you asked me if Emma was out of my life, my friends thought that you were making sure I was emotionally available and wasn't going back before you got more involved."

Marina responded, "That's because your friends are men."

I tried to respond as kindly as I could. "Both of the friends I asked were women."

That seemed to make an impression.

"I've just never met anyone like you," she said. "You're so passionate, intense, and unpredictable sometimes. I don't know how to deal with it."

I laughed and said, "I'm an artist! Artists are not normal people like everyone else. We do everything in more dramatic ways. You should *see* some of my musician friends. I'm the most normal one in the bunch!"

We both laughed. This lightened up the conversation.

I continued, "But you don't understand what it's like to travel out of town every week to work. Then you count down the days until you get home. I couldn't understand why you wouldn't pick up the phone and talk to me. I do understand that you haven't been sleeping well because of your insomnia. It must be contagious because I have it now as well."

Marina smiled.

"While I was on the flight home, I went into meditation and had this deep spiritual experience. It was such a shock waking up and then being so disappointed when you cancelled our getting together. There was so much nice energy going on between us last week. I hate for this to end on such a sour note. I think we both did some things that weren't right. Can we just put this behind us and try to forget this ever happened?"

I spoke from the heart and she softened a little.

A Beatles song began to play in the background and she changed the subject. "What's been the high point of your career?"

I didn't have to ponder that very long. "When Paul McCartney started a standing ovation for me."

"That's exciting! Tell me what happened."

So I told her the story.

Chapter 15

Sir Paul, Heather, and the Standing Ovation

Ialways had a great appreciation for Paul McCartney, and I wondered how I could get some of my music to him after his beloved first wife Linda passed away. Despite the fact that he's very famous, he's still a human being. I felt that peaceful, relaxing music could help him heal through his grieving process.

I had a lot of contacts in the music and entertainment business when I was living in Los Angeles, but no one I knew at the time had a connection with Paul McCartney. A few months of dead-end phone calls later, I let go of the idea of finding him. I just surrendered it to Spirit.

Inwardly, I said, *God, I put this into your hands. If it is meant for Paul to have some of my music to help him heal, then may the blessings be.* I imagined this thought being lifted up from my hands, sailing up to the sky and out to the heavens.

I forgot about it and life went on.

Six months later, I got a call from the Atlanta Wholesale Gift Show. I was scheduled to have a booth at the show in January to sell my music, and they were asking how much I'd charge to perform at a corporate event connected to the gift show. I quoted her a price, and the woman on the phone said my price was more than what they wanted to pay.

Then we spoke about the arrangements for my booth at the gift show—the location, table and chairs, electricity, etc. As she continued to fill me in on the technical information, I had this nagging feeling to ask her who the corporate event was for, which was unusual. Normally, after you give someone a quote, the conversation is over if it's not in the budget. But I asked anyway, following the nudge of Divine Inner Guidance.

"Heather McCartney, Paul McCartney's daughter," she said.

"Is Paul McCartney going to be there?" I couldn't resist asking.

"I'm really not sure," she answered.

"When is the event?" I queried.

"It's the night before the gift show starts," she replied. I was booked for the show anyway, and I only had to get there one night earlier.

"What is your budget for music at the event?" I asked her.

She told me her budget, I thought about it, then said, "I'll do it."

My wife at the time and I went to the airport the next day and had the tickets changed. When I told them why I was changing the flight dates, they waived the change fee and wished me good luck.

We flew to Atlanta for the gigantic gift show that filled three buildings downtown. The McCartney organization had a large showroom on one of the higher floors, displaying all of Heather's designs: plates, rugs, and various gift items with a Southwestern flair. When Heather was a child, her family spent summer vacations outside Tucson, Arizona. She was influenced by the colorful styles of the local artisans there.

I was to play music inside the main entrance of the showroom at the event. The press conference and her artwork were in the room across from me. People crowded the halls, causing quite a huge buzz in the building.

From where I was standing, I could see Paul, Heather, and their bodyguard through the large showroom windows. They started walking down the hall past the other showrooms toward me. I'd never seen so many women in their forties, fifties, and sixties losing it as if they were teenage girls!

When they finally got to the doorway, Paul pointed to me and said to Heather, "Hey, look, the flute guy is here." They both waved to me as if we were all old friends. That was surreal. The event coordinator must have sent them one of my CDs in advance.

The press was all over them immediately, cameras and microphones in the air, firing a flurry of questions at them, trying for an interview. This was Paul's first public appearance since Linda had passed away six months earlier, and every major TV network, newspaper, and magazine was there. Another day in the life of a Beatle, but this was a little different. He had adopted Heather when she was only three years old, and he was there to support her work.

The funny thing was that Paul seemed to be very interested and amused that I was playing two flutes at one time in harmony. His entourage attempted to get them through to the press room for approximately fifteen minutes, all the time right in front of where I was playing. Paul kept reaching his head up to see over everyone else, trying to figure out how I was doing what I was doing and smiling at me the whole time. Eventually, they did make it over to the other side where the press conference was to be held.

My mind still reeled from the friendly vibes I got from Paul and Heather. They made me feel like I was one of them, part of their entourage. The family videographer kept smiling, and came over to film me a number of times.

One young guy in his twenties wearing a surfer beanie really stuck out in the 45- to 75-year-old crowd at the event. I wondered what he was doing there, but most of all I was wondering why he kept hitting on my wife at the time. (I'm not a jealous guy, but apparently he wasn't aware that she was with me.) He would also chat with the family videographer each time he came by to film me, and I finally realized that this was Heather's brother, James.

I decided to ask my wife to get one of my CDs so I could sign it and give it to James as a gift for Heather. (That would also give him a second to realize that he'd been hitting on my wife.) I signed the cover of the CD "To Heather, Best of Luck, David Young." After James saw me kiss my wife and get the CD from her, he disappeared. I didn't see him again for the remainder of the event.

Eventually, the press conference ended and mania followed Paul and Heather back across the room as they were trying to leave. The best way I can describe what I saw was a swarm of bees buzzing around a nest. People were flipping out trying to get Paul's autograph. Sounds of hysteria and excitement filled the air. The entourage had to cross to my side of the room once again to exit the main door. It struck me that we were likely going to get one last chance to make eye contact and say goodbye. Nothing in Paul's life happens quickly; just getting across the room took twenty minutes.

Finally there they were, right in front of me. Paul suddenly stopped to talk to me and quieted down the whole crowd. The room was instantly silent.

He looked at me, smiled, and said, "Very well done."

"Thank you very much, Sir," I replied.

Time stood still. I'd called him "Sir" out of respect for him as a musician. He had just been knighted and seemed surprised to have an American call him "Sir." He wore a curious look on his face.

"This was extremely well-done, but you're not getting the praise you so deserve," he said. He then started clapping for me. The whole crowd joined in, figuring that since Paul McCartney appreciated my music, they had better applaud as well.

I remembered then that I'd signed a CD to give to Heather's brother, but since he'd disappeared, I still had it. I reached over, picked it up and handed it to Paul. When he saw that it was signed, "To Heather, Best of Luck, David Young," he gave me a curious look—as if I'd just performed a magic trick. I could practically read Paul's thoughts. He was probably thinking, how did I come up with a personally signed CD without him seeing me sign it?

Then I said, "This is for Heather because it's her special day." He was very happy that I put the spotlight back on her, and he strongly shook my hand. Then they left.

Once the event was over, Paul's manager approached me and said, "I can't tell you how many times Paul remarked on how much he liked your music. He truly thought it was great." Seeing the style of Heather's art, I had chosen to play all songs with a Native American flavor.

"I enjoyed your music, too," the manager continued, "and if you could give me a CD for myself, I'd also be happy to give one to Paul."

I've told this story many times since, but it wasn't until a year later that I remembered my first intention was to give Paul one of my CDs for healing when his wife Linda had passed away. And even though I wasn't able to find anyone to get my music to Paul McCartney, spirit found a way for me to give my music to him directly—from my hand to his.

"What an amazing story!" Marina said. "Did you know that George Harrison used to baby-sit me?" Marina asked.

"What did you say?"

"George Harrison used to baby-sit me when I was a kid," she repeated.

"Do you want to tell me a little more about that?" I asked.

I flashed back to the memory of listening to "Within You Without You" over and over in my car, and the DVD of *The Concert for Bangladesh* in my friend's house and the cassette tape popping up the same day in my other friend's van. I tried to keep my composure, but my mind was reeling.

Marina continued. "Mom and George studied under the same guru in Tuscon, Arizona, and met when she separated from my dad. She and George got together and fell in love. Eventually he moved Mom and me to England to live in his castle, and that's where I grew up."

"Do you know that people have been comparing my music to his for the past two years because my lyrics are spiritual? I had a couple of really bizarre things happen a few months ago that made me feel like he was trying to communicate with me."

This didn't seem to make much of an impression on her, but inside I was flipping out, thinking, *This woman is filled with surprises!*

After more small talk, we left the coffee shop and walked to my car. Out of the blue, Marina asked, "So when am I going to hear this 'ridiculously beautiful' song you told me about?"

"I don't know. I need to find a studio around here to work in," I replied. We stood and continued chatting on the street corner by my car. Since she was standing on the lower side of the curb, I noticed that, at that moment, I was a little taller than she. We said goodbye, and as she began to walk away I said, "Wait a minute, can you do that again?"

"Do what again?"

"Stand where you just were over there." I pointed to the lower spot on the curb. She stepped back there, making me taller than her again. Before she realized what was happening, I quickly kissed her on the lips.

She smiled, then walked away.

Chapter 16

Story Time with DAY (David A. Young)

Marina and I had a short conversation the following day, and I don't know why, but I suddenly found myself asking, "Do you like to play tennis?"

Marina looked startled, "Oh, my gosh, I'm supposed to be at my first tennis lesson in fifteen minutes! I don't know why you thought to ask me that, but I have to go."

As soon as I arrived home, I had to write the following email to bring closure to our truncated conversation.

▲▲▲

From: David
To: Marina
Subject: George Harrison
Date: Wed, 20 Oct 2010 07:28:33

Hi Marina,

I wanted to tell you more about why I was so affected by the news you shared about George Harrison being your babysitter when you were little.

After I started blending spirituality and rock music, some have commented that some of my music is reminiscent of George Harrison. People have actually written to me saying that I was "carrying the torch that George Harrison carried." That is such a meaningful, beautiful compliment and a deep honor. This has happened so many times over the last few years that I actually started to listen to his music so I could understand why. I guess if there was anything we had in common, besides dark hair and dark eyes, it's that we both started out playing rock music with electric guitars, and somewhere down the road of life we each found spirituality and meditation and then tried to communicate something deeper or spiritual through our music.

In my opinion, the three saddest moments in modern music history were the day John Lennon was shot, the day John Bonham died, and the day I found out that George Harrison was sued for his song "My Sweet Lord." It broke my heart when I heard that he had lost that lawsuit.

There are two ways to write a song:
1) to make the words rhyme, or

2) because you have something important to say and you use the song as the carrier for your message.

From being a spiritual person, I think I understand why George wrote that song. The words, "I really want to see you, I really want to be with you. I really want to see you Lord, but it takes so long, my Lord" are about longing to have a real spiritual experience with the Creator. The problem is that it takes so long to quiet the mind and get into the higher consciousness of Soul to do that.

For some reason that I don't know, I have had numerous connections with people who have known or worked with the Beatles. I will tell you these sometime and we can share them with your mom if she would like to hear them.

Namasté,
David

From: Marina
To: David
Subject: RE: - George Harrison
Date: Wed, 20 Oct 2010 12:55:19

Wow, so very interesting . . . I like your emails . . . I feel like it's "Story time with David A. Young."

I would definitely like to share your experiences and stories surrounding the Beatles and George Harrison, specifically with my mom. Undoubtedly, she would enjoy them . . . as I have . . . but in a deeper way as she spent meaningful time with the man.

Thanks again for the tennis reminder, although that was not your intention.

Enjoy the rest of your day, DAY :) I like saying that . . . and I look forward to hearing the "ridiculously beautiful" song one of these days.

Kindly,
Marina

Marina and I made plans to get together a few days later but she cancelled at the last minute, frustrating me again. The radio played . . . .

One of us is vulnerable, it's not you
One of us is touchable, it's not you
One of us is available, one of us is attainable
One of us is vulnerable and it's not you
One of us is a mystery, and it's not me
One of us has hidden history, it's not me
One of us is attainable, one of us is available
One of us is vulnerable and it's not you

It had been weeks now since I'd slept well. Up every night playing that ridiculously beautiful song for hours and practicing, I was getting ready for an upcoming concert that was about a week away.

Marina kept telling me to have patience with her process and that the more I pushed to get together with her, the more she wanted to pull away.

I struggle with patience, even in easier circumstances. By this time the song felt like an infant ready for birth. The only way to accomplish this was to record it. Since I was new to the area, I didn't know of any recording studios. Stephanie, my friend from Yogaphoria, mentioned she had a friend with a professional studio, but she never followed up with the information. This added to my frustration since I was used to having so many high-quality studios at my disposal in Minneapolis.

A friend gave me the idea to do a Google search to find a recording studio. There were two: Cambridge Sound Studios in Newtown, Pennsylvania and August Moon Recording in Pennington. I called Cambridge first, but they were booked up for ten days. When I called August Moon to find available studio time, John the studio owner asked, "How soon can you get here?"

I said, "I can leave for your place right now."

John said, "I can be ready for you in twenty minutes."

I gratefully responded, "That is exactly what I wanted to hear."

I had no idea where Pennington was, but loaded up my car with guitars and amps, then entered the address in my GPS. By now, I was almost frantic to get this song out of me.

I also felt if there was anything that could get Marina off the fence once and for all, this would be it. As I drove, I realized that I was headed in the same direction as Marina's place. Pennington is the next town over.

I arrived at a nice house in a suburban residential neighborhood. John was in his mid-fifties with a grayish beard and ruffled hair. The studio was in the basement. There were guitar cases everywhere. John is also a guitar collector, with over 150 vintage guitars. This was like heaven on earth for a guitar player. His equipment, which was mainly used as his home studio to record his own music, was almost as old as the guitars. This stuff was out of date fifteen years ago! Nothing was digital or computerized, but my needs were very basic. I only wanted to record a vocal and a guitar on this song. It didn't have to be fancy.

And so I recorded "The Key to Your Heart."

After the recording was complete, I asked John to make an MP3 of it so I could send it to Marina via email. I didn't want to contact her anymore or put myself in a more vulnerable position than I was already in. John's equipment was so out of date, though, that he couldn't do it. However, he could burn a CD of the song that I could take with me, but that meant I had to drop it off—which I didn't want to do.

After the copy was made, Peter, one of my new friends, called. During our conversation, I casually asked for his opinion of what to do. I didn't know if I had the courage to leave it in her mailbox. I'd felt pretty vulnerable up to this point, and giving her this song made me feel even more vulnerable. I'd been pretty adept in the past in connecting with women over the past twenty years, so I was not used to this uncomfortable feeling.

Trying to convince myself, I told Peter, "I am sort of psychic. I saw the housing market crash five years before it happened. I anticipated the stock market crash six months before it happened. And I know she has feelings for me."

Peter offered to take the drive with me, and we drove around for an hour before finally agreeing that I had nothing to lose. It was about 11:00 p.m. when we arrived at her house. Peter waited in the car while I jumped out and slipped it into her mailbox. As we drove off, I texted her, "The ridiculously beautiful song is in your mailbox now."

Chapter 17

The Key to Your Heart

You're a woman of integrity; I'm a man of integrity
You're a woman of sincerity and I'm a man with this quality
The more of you that I see,
the more I believe we are destined to be
But I can't wait forever but I'll wait for you now
'Til I find the key to your heart
With sincerity and honesty, integrity, and harmony
I'll find the key to your heart
I won't let you down; I will never let you down
And I won't stop looking 'til I find the
key to your heart

I know you've been hurt before,
as many times as I have been hurt
But I'm willing to give this a chance
and risk opening my heart once more
I know I have a lot to give and
I want to love you as long as I live

But I can't wait forever but I'll wait for you now
'Til I find the key to your heart
With sincerity and honesty, integrity, and harmony
I'll find the key to your heart
I won't let you down; I will never let you down
And I won't stop looking 'til I find the key to your heart

▲ ▲ ▲

Marina called me the following morning and had already listened to the song ten times.

She was blown away. "It is so beautiful! How could you do that so fast?"

I responded, "This is what I do."

She was incredibly appreciative and touched beyond words by what I gave her.

"I want to give you something back for this incredible gift. Can I make you more soup?" she asked.

"That would be great," I answered.

"Since you have given me so much of your yoga music and now this song, I will give you as much soup as you want until 2015!"

We agreed on a time to get together so she could give me some soup and we could chat as friends. I had no intention of making any moves on her. She'd convinced me she could not love anyone right now.

I picked her up at her house and we went for a ride, finding a tree with the most incredible autumn leaves changing on it. I told her about my big concert coming up the following Saturday night and she said she wanted to bring Zarina to it. Zarina was enthralled that a man had written and recorded a song for her mom. Marina had been playing it about thirty times a day since I'd dropped it off. Marina said, "My next-door neighbor has heard the song played so many times that she is singing along when I play it now."

Later that evening, I sent this email to her.

▲ ▲ ▲

From: David
To: Marina
Subject: The Song

It was nice hanging with you today and parking next to the most beautiful tree in the park. It was good to discuss the things we spoke of, too. You know, even though our relationship was mostly friendship, we have managed to have a child together somehow—the song. I could not have written it without you, and I don't think you could have written it without me either.

With the state of the music business being what it is, I don't know where the song will go—whether it will be heard by many people, or enjoyed by just a few. I'd sworn I would never write another song when I left Minneapolis, but I love writing and recording. The universe picked you to inspire my heart again. You are a beautiful person, and a gift to all fortunate enough to be around you. I mean that. If you are ever having a hard day, remember this. I'll play football on your team anytime!

We were talking about past lives today, and after seeing how fond of you I became in such a short amount of time, I would guess that we've crossed paths in some other time and place.

There were good vibes already between us. I liked you instantly. So sweet dreams to you and if you wear out that CD, I will get another one for you. I am glad that I finally got to write words to the most favorite piece of music that I have ever written. I play it just about every time I pick my guitar up. I used to wonder why I couldn't find the right words for that piece of music, but now it is a musical picture of how wonderful you are to me.

With love,
David

Chapter 18

Zarina, Zarina, Zarina

As the weeks went by, my head cleared to the point where I was feeling back to my normal self. Monica, Lisa's friend, and I had a few nice conversations and planned to get together, but her best friend became deathly ill so she had to cancel.

The Sugarloaf Art Festival was scheduled for Somerset, New Jersey, on Halloween weekend. Since I'd run out of soup, I texted Marina that I'd be available to pick some up Sunday night after the show was over. When I arrived, Marina invited me in and we sat on the couch enjoying some nice conversation. Whether we liked it or not, there was a bond between us. Maybe it was the song, maybe it was our history or the chemistry, but there was something there. The room just felt energized when we were together, and I could see she felt it too.

Zarina was very happy to see me. The concert was coming up and she was really looking forward to it. Since it was the night before Halloween, Marina asked Zarina to put on her costume to show me. As she walked down the steps in a little angel outfit, it was like my world went into slow motion. My heart melted. I was pulled back into the whole thing all over again.

Later that night at home, with insomnia still keeping me awake, I wrote the song "Zarina."

Soft, white,
in an angel's dress,
that's my vision of Zarina.
I wait on the couch
for my little ballerina.
Then she appears,
Oh, I wish you could have seen her,
Zarina ...
Zarina ... Zarina ...
Zarina ... Zarina ...

▲▲▲

I finally did fall asleep, but when the morning came, the song was still burning in me so I called the studio.

"Hey, John, I have another song. Can I record it this afternoon?" I asked.

"Sure, the studio is open today," he responded.

I added drums, bass, acoustic, electric, and a lead guitar to the vocals on this song. It was a bigger production than the first one, so I multi-tracked the background vocals to sound like a giant chorus singing Zarina's name. The song was finished around midnight. I drove to Marina's house with the full moon overhead, walked up the porch steps, and dropped the second song in their mailbox. I suspected that none of our lives would ever be the same.

Zarina was such a unique name that she was never able to find trinkets with her name on it the way other little girls could. This song struck home like a beautiful atom bomb in their lives. Whatever feelings Zarina had for me multiplied by a thousand. The problem now for Marina was that she was outnumbered. Her strong-willed little daughter only wanted to know, "When is David coming over again?" "David, David, David . . . ."

Chapter 19

And Still I Wait

Now there were two of these new songs that played each day in their house. Marina was trying her best to keep me out of her heart. She told me, "If you really have the feelings you say you have for me, which you have written about in such loving detail in your songs, then you will have the patience to give me time."

I was still unsure she would ever let me in. This drove me to write and record the song "And Still I Wait."

▲ ▲ ▲

I don't know what you think but I know how I feel
I'm not sure what you want but I want something real
You and I have been together long enough to know
And when I want to talk about it you just let it go
You just say, "Let's wait until tomorrow"

That's what you say every day
And so I say, "I'll wait until tomorrow"
Just like I did yesterday, and still I wait

I have said so many things but still I don't understand
If you and I have this harmony, then why don't we
just make a plan
You and I have been together long enough to know
Let's find a place to live together and watch
our garden grow
You just say, "Let's wait until tomorrow"
That's what you say every day
And so I say, "I'll wait until tomorrow"
Just like I did yesterday, and still I wait

Chapter 20

I'm Still Missing You

The following weekend, at another festival, these words came to me out of the blue while I was performing. I was playing one song on my flute in my left hand and wrote these lyrics with my right hand. It was almost impossible to do the two at once.

I wish I really knew what life was all about
Why some people have so much and others live without
I wish I had a dream that really did come true.
But I really wish I knew why I'm still missing you

I wish I really knew why this world has so much pain.
Why we live and why we die and then do it all again.
And if I ever understand all the struggles
I've been through,
Then maybe I'll understand why I'm still missing you

I wish I really knew why so many people cry.
Oh, I wish that I could sing the world a lullaby.
If we all helped one person, the good that we could do
And then maybe I'd find a way to stop missing you

▲▲▲

Normally, my lyrics immediately turned into songs with music, but not this one. The paper I'd scribbled them on sat on the dresser in my bedroom for days.

The night of the concert arrived and there was a full house. As I performed, I alternated between singing and playing guitar, telling stories, and playing the flutes.

Zarina beamed, sitting on her mom's lap, wearing a tie-dyed T-shirt with a peace sign on it. Marina didn't appear to be very comfortable—like she was just along for the ride. Maybe she was afraid that I was going to dedicate a song to her, and thinking, *Who knows what he'll do next at this point?*

During intermission, Zarina ran up to me and gave me a huge hug.

Marina complimented me, "Great performance. You're like Bruce Springsteen with boundless energy. I don't know if we will be able to stay through the whole second set. It's getting late and Zarina needs to get to bed soon." Zarina boldly spoke up, "We'll leave when I'm ready to leave, Mom."

Halfway through the second set, I announced to the audience, "Tonight, for the first time, I'm going to sing a special song that I didn't write. But it really means a lot to me." I sang "My Sweet Lord." To my amazement, the audience sang along in beautiful harmony. It was the high point of the show.

When the song ended, I looked around, but Marina and Zarina were not there. The concert was a big success. After signing numerous autographs, I went home only feeling about half as elated as I could have.

I awoke in the middle of the night with a nudge to pick up the lyrics still sitting on my dresser. As I read the words, I wondered once again how the heck the music should go for lyrics like this.

At the exact moment the thought finished going through my head, someone started playing the guitar just to the right of my bed. The notes were loud and clear. The pattern was played twice. There was no sound anywhere else in the house. I was alone. I felt prickles on my neck.

Is this a ghost? I wondered. I hoped not. "Don't be a ghost," I said. "I'm scared shitless of ghosts!" But I picked up my guitar, anyway, and out of all of the possible notes I could have played, my fingers went exactly to the correct notes the ghost just played for me. The riff went perfectly with the unfinished lyrics on the paper. I recorded it on my little tape deck and fell back asleep.

The following morning I added these words for the bridge of the song.

Every time I think I really have moved on
And my head is finally clear and my feelings
for you are gone
Life brings me down your street and
I'm seeing you again
And the cycle starts all over, and I am missing you.
I'm still missing you

I called John at the studio, and fortunately the studio was free once again. I arranged to record at 10:00 a.m. This song was different from the others. It was more up-tempo and the nice beat kept it moving. While I was recording the first electric guitar part with my headphones on in the booth (John was in the next room), this thought ran through my mind: *This part sounds so much like something George Harrison would have written.*

At that exact moment, a little blue star enveloped by a huge glowing blue light appeared in the booth and lit up the whole right side of the room. It was spectacular! It pulsed and sparkled like nothing I'd ever seen. I knew this was George's spirit confirming my suspicions. His light hovered there for six seconds. A huge feeling of love embraced me as I continued to play.

After recording the track, I started adding other instruments: bass, drums, vocals, and harmony vocals. A powerful creative energy was driving me on. Since the guitar part was not something I would have written myself, it wasn't in my typical style. I added twelve tracks of other guitars to try to blend the sounds together to establish a distinct new tone. I drove John out of his mind during the process of playing it over so many times.

I'd made a little mistake in the arrangement while distracted by George's light and lost track of where I was in the song. Now the middle section was too long. Since the studio was analog, this couldn't be shortened digitally, so I figured I'd edit it out later in the mastering process.

Once the vocals and all the other instruments were added and mixed, I left the studio to go to a music store. I had to repair one of my PA systems that I would need for the gigs I had coming up. As I listened to the song in the car, I realized that the tone and sound of the guitar still wasn't right. I called John to tell him I needed to come back and use one of his vintage guitars.

"Come on, David, have you totally lost it? You've already laid down twelve tracks of that same part!" But in the end, John agreed to let me come back.

I arrived at the music store, and for some bizarre reason their stereo was blasting loud. I found a repairman who tried to fix my broken PA system, but he was unable to figure it out. "Why don't you pick out a loaner system you can borrow until your system is fixed by the factory?"

The tech guy sent a salesman over to help me plug one in so I could check the sound. This should have taken about ten seconds to plug in, but the salesman couldn't get it to work. During that whole time, the music on the store's PA system was so loud it was difficult to hear each other talk.

After fifteen minutes of messing around with the wires, the salesman finally got the PA to work. He handed me a microphone to try the system and walked away. At that exact moment, the song on the store's music system changed and George Harrison's song "Give Me Love (Give Me Peace on Earth)" came blasting on. I stood there holding the microphone. For a moment, I was speechless. Since I was supposed to be checking the speakers, I sang along with the whole song. Everyone else in the store had disappeared. When it was over, I found the salesman in the back and arranged to borrow the loaner system.

I left the store and headed back to the studio, contemplating all of the incredible things that happened so far that day. When I returned to the studio, I said to John, "I know I've driven you crazy recording twelve tracks of this guitar part already, but I need a cleaner, more bell-tone sound. Since you have so many guitars, could you suggest one for me?"

There were guitar cases everywhere in his house and studio. You couldn't even sit on the couch because its space was taken up with five more guitars. John walked in and out of different rooms for about ten minutes, then came back with a beat-up old case. He laid it on the floor by my feet and opened it up. It was so old it didn't have any finish or paint on it.

Having never seen one of these before, I asked John, "What is it?"

"It's a 1955 Gretsch." I kept staring at the old relic, prompting John to add, "It's the George Harrison model. It's the same model guitar George used in the Beatles, except the one George played was a 1958."

John had no idea what had already happened that day. I went into the recording booth with George's guitar and played the song that George wrote with me. It was the perfect sound.

After the session, I texted Marina. "Three miracles happened today."

"I can't wait to hear them," she wrote back.

Chapter 21

More Soup

The next day I called Marina. It was time for more soup again. Since the studio was close to her house, I asked if she could meet me there. The new song was all cued up for when she arrived.

I was very excited to share the incredible events of the previous day, but when she arrived with the soup, she just wanted to drop it off and leave. I finally was able to convince her to stay for just a few minutes to hear the new song. I just couldn't contain my excitement. Hesitantly, she left her car running and walked with me downstairs to the studio.

After playing the song for her, I asked, "Well, what do you think?" I was very proud of this song, and couldn't wait to tell her about the three miracles.

Marina replies, "I like the beat and the catchy chorus of 'I'm Still Missing You,' but I think the middle section is too long and boring." (That was the part where George had appeared as the light and I lost my sense of time.)

Then she said, "But I don't think you're missing me enough."

"What?"

"It doesn't sound like you're missing me enough," she repeated.

At that point, Marina became very embarrassed because we'd already had so many miscommunications in emails and texts. Now she realized that she had just told me that I wasn't "missing her enough."

Perhaps thinking she had insulted my music as well, Marina said, "But I don't know anything about music. I've got to go!"

"Wait a minute," I said with all the calm I could muster, "What are you trying to say? I appreciate your taste in music, and I want to understand what you mean."

She hesitated for another second, then said, "It doesn't sound like you really mean it when you sing 'I'm Still Missing You.' As a listener, I can't believe you. There's not enough emotion in your voice to really convince me you're sincere. And that middle part is just way too long."

After that, she practically ran out of the studio. I called to John, "Hook up the microphone, I'm going to sing some ad-libs in that middle section she said was too long." John rolled his eyes.

Then I blasted that song with so much emotion and power it's amazing the microphone didn't blow up! But it was exactly what the song needed.

Afterwards, I texted Marina when the song was finished. "I think I'm missing you enough now."

Marina texted back, "You made me crack up. That's hilarious!"

I paid John's bill for the studio time, and as I was leaving the studio, I texted her, "Congratulations, you win the award. I've never tried so hard to get someone to love me back, only to have failed miserably."

Immediately, she texted back, "I don't want that award!"

I had to respond. "I have such a love for you and Zarina, and I wish you could receive it. I so want to be a family with you." It struck me that I had essentially just said "I love you" to her.

"I care about you, too," Marina texted. "I have just been in such an awful place in my heart. I haven't been able to receive any of what you have been trying to give me. I wish I was in a different place."

I wrote back, "I am leaving for twelve days to drive to North Carolina and I wish I could come over and kiss you goodbye before I go." At this point, I figured I had nothing to lose and was convinced that, after "the three miracles," that George was doing everything possible to get us together.

Marina replies, "Okay, I'll call you after I put Zarina to bed. If you come over while she's awake, she won't want to go to sleep."

Is she finally letting me in? Is the dragon giving up?

I drove back to my apartment and showed my roommate the text. "You see, I told you that she really has feelings for me. You won't believe what has happened in the past twenty-four hours!" I recounted the events of the incredible day.

Marina suddenly texted, "Zarina is getting tired, and I will let you know in about forty-five minutes when you should leave to come over."

I laid down on my bed smiling. My cell phone was right next to my ear, waiting for her text. Since I hadn't slept well in weeks, I fell into a deep sleep and didn't hear the message come in. "She's asleep so you can come over now."

I woke up four hours later, saw the message, and realized I had missed the opportunity to finally be with her.

I texted, "OMG! I fell asleep and just woke up at 2:30 a.m. I have to drive nine hours to North Carolina now! Please call me when you get up."

Chapter 22

One-Woman Man

While driving south on the highway, I held the steering wheel with my left hand and with my right hand wrote the song "One-Woman Man" on a notepad. Then I sang it into my little hand-held tape recorder so I could remember the melody.

I've been looking for a woman to treat me nice
I'm not looking for a sugar mama in paradise
And I've met a lot of women that just weren't right
So do you want to be my woman?
My one and only woman?
Do you want to be the woman for this one-woman man?

I have met a lot of women who have done me wrong
And I'm getting tired of singing that sad, sad song
But I need a tender woman to who my heart can belong

I'm just looking for one woman
One warm tender woman
Do you want to be the woman for this one-woman man?

You are a diamond waiting to be found
I'm not scamming women like every guy in this town
My ego is fine without chasing around and around
I just wanna love and be loved
So do you wanna be the woman for this one-woman man?

I was singing as a state trooper suddenly showed up behind me with his siren singing and lights flashing to pull me over. The officer walked up to the passenger window of my car and asked in his thick Southern accent, "Do you realize you were drivin' above the posted speed limit?"

"I realize it now that you've pulled me over," I answered.

The officer cracked a smile. I noticed the name on his badge.

"Your last name is Klein? That's my uncle's last name."

"Really? What county's he from?" His strong accent was an auditory shock to my ears.

"Brooklyn," I replied.

"Not sure where that is. License and registration, please," Officer Klein kindly asked.

I handed them to him and he walked back to his car.

I called Marina. "Good morning."

"How's the drive going?" she asked in a sleepy voice.

"I'm halfway to Charlotte, and there's good news and bad news. The good news is that I've written another beautiful song for you."

"Aww, that's nice," she responded warmly. "You're my musical entertainment man."

"The bad news is that I just got pulled over for speeding."

"Oh, darn."

"I still need to tell you about the three miracles that happened yesterday."

In the rearview mirror, I could see the state trooper walking back towards me with a ticket.

"Talk with you later. I gotta go now."

Officer Klein leaned into my window and asked, "Where are you going in such a hurry, Mister Young?"

"I'm performing at the Holiday Christmas Show in Charlotte."

"Really, yer a musician?"

"Yes I am, sir."

"Well, I'm a singer myself. What instrument do you play?"

"I'm a singer and guitar player, but I'm actually known for playing two flutes at one time," I replied.

The trooper's interest was piqued. "Really. Well, how do ya do that?"

"I put one in my left hand and one in my right hand."

"Well, I'll be darned. Never heard a' that before. Do ya have one a' those websites I can look your music up on?" he asks.

"I sure do, sir. You have my name now, so you can just look me up."

"That's right, I *sure* do." He handed me the ticket, continuing the conversation.

"I like to write country songs and I came in second place last month at a little competition in my hometown. Maybe I can send you some songs for ya to listen ta."

"That would be great," I smiled, playing along. "I'm a songwriter as well. Actually the reason why I was speeding is because I was writing a song for this woman I really like. I was recording it on my little tape deck so I wouldn't lose the melody."

The officer seriously notes, "Well, that's a good way to do it. If yer not drivin'."

I looked down and saw that my red recorder light was still on. I had to laugh. "Oh, my God! I forgot to turn it off when you pulled me over and it's been recording our whole conversation!"

"Let me hear a l'il bit of the song," said Trooper Klein. "Let's see if she's any good."

I rewound the tape as I laughed, then pressed the Play button. Trooper Klein leaned his head inside the car window a little further so he could hear it better.

I replayed the song:

I've been looking for a woman to treat me nice,
I'm not looking for a sugar mama in paradise . . .

Trooper Klein remarked, impressed, "That's *good*, that's *real* good."

Raising his eyebrows, he added, "She's gonna really like that one. *Mmm mmm!*"

Trooper Klein straightened up and fixed his shirt. "Well, have yourself a nice day, Mister Young. And slow down and drive safe, ya hear?"

Chapter 23

Gotta Get Close to You

Iarrived in Charlotte, North Carolina for the Southern Christmas Show, one of the largest events of the year with over 1,200 booths. The show hours are 9 a.m. to 9 p.m., so I hired an assistant to help work the evening hours for me during the slow time so I could go to another recording studio at night. Since I'd written five more songs that week, "One-Woman Man," "Helpless," "Gotta Get Close to You," "One Look," and "My Dear Friend," I did a Google search to find another recording studio.

There was a great vibe in the texts I shared with Marina now. I invited her and Zarina to spend Thanksgiving with me and my family in northern New Jersey. She accepted! The last song had convinced her to trust me in a deeper way than before. Although I'd slept through my opportunity to be with her, she finally opened the door and let me in. This brought me inner peace, as well as excitement. It was appearing that

George Harrison was now like a guardian angel to me. It gave me renewed confidence in myself and my music.

Over the past few weeks, I'd been increasing my daily meditations from thirty minutes to sixty and then ninety minutes. It was lifting me up to a higher level of spiritual awareness. My intuition was heightened. I was in a much happier place.

Something truly unique happened on my third morning in Charlotte. In fact, it's something I'd never experienced before. After about forty-five minutes of meditating, I was in a state of deep bliss. A woman with dark brown hair and an amazing smile flew directly into the inner vision in my third eye, kissed me right on the lips, and then disappeared. I knew I'd seen her somewhere before, but wasn't sure where. My only guess was that it could've been Stephanie, from Yogaphoria. But that certainly didn't seem like something she would do. The jolt of this experience brought me out of meditation.

I immediately got out of bed, turned on my laptop, and discovered a Facebook message from Stephanie. "Are you okay? When are you back in town? Call me. My relationship status has been changed to single."

What insane timing! But I stayed focused on the good vibes with Marina and, later in the day, sent her this text: "What do you think about the idea of flying down to Charlotte Friday and staying until Sunday? It would give us some time to be together. I looked at the flights, and we can get a good price if we buy it now. The show is going to be busy over the weekend and I can use some extra help." After sending the text, I went to the studio and recorded "Gotta Get Close to You."

It feels so good and I've got it bad
This is the craziest kinda love I ever had
I can't think and I can't sleep
I've been the Energizer bunny for over a week
Give me a tip, just give me a clue
Tell me what I need to get over or under you
'Cuz I gotta get close to you, I gotta get close to you
Tell me what I what I gotta do to make you love me

Chapter 24

Miscommunication

I left the studio at 2:00 a.m., and drove back to my hotel to crash. At 8:00 a.m., I woke up to a text from Marina.

"How can you buy a ticket for me without asking me first? How do you expect me to drop everything and fly down there to help you? That is so consistent with your pushy aggressiveness. The whole world doesn't revolve around you."

I tried to stay calm, not really sure where any of this was coming from. Everything was wonderful with us the night before.

RROOAARR! said the dragon . . . .

"Wait a minute," I wrote back. "I didn't buy tickets. I just meant that we'd need to act no more than twenty-four hours in advance, or else it would be much more expensive."

Marina continued. "And how can you go to a show without help and expect me to work for you last-minute? Don't you plan these things in advance?"

I responded, "I have already hired an assistant down here who's been helping me. If it gets super-busy over the weekend at peak hours, you could work for me if you wanted to. If not, there's so much to see at the show. You can just walk around and enjoy yourself."

She continued. "And how do you know that I have coverage for Zarina. You are so self-centered! And I don't like the way you speak to her. How could you ask her for a hug like that, the last time you were here?"

I explained. "Yesterday, you told me that Zarina would be spending the weekend with her dad and that you had nothing planned. I was just offering to fly you down here so you wouldn't be alone. We could have some nice time together without you having any distractions or responsibilities."

"Oh, I didn't understand that," Marina admitted.

"That's why I wrote that you should call me so I could explain it to you. All this texting and emailing is ridiculous. There would be much less miscommunication if we talked more and texted less."

By this time, I realized that each time Marina opened up and let me in, her dragon of fear and doubt reared its ugly head and sabotaged our harmony. It's not that she was being mean. I just felt that she was so afraid of getting hurt again. The energy between us then was so negative that both our cell phones jammed, deleting all of our messages from the past month.

Marina texted, "Oh, my God, all of our messages have been deleted!"

Why do you even care about our messages when you keep telling me that you don't have any feelings for me? I wondered. "I think I've had enough of this," I wrote back.

Chapter 25

I've Given Up: I Can't Save You from You

I finished the twelve days at the festival and drove home to Pennsylvania. In frustration, I wrote the song "I've Given Up" as I drove.

Each time I think we're getting on track
You move one step closer then take ten steps back
Each time I think we're getting on track
You move one step closer then take ten steps back
There comes a time when we all have to say
I've given enough, I've given enough
Our timing wasn't right and you couldn't love
Now I've given up, I've given up
Some people say that love conquers all
I'd like to believe it's true
But to those you believe that love conquers all

I say that's 'cuz they never met you
They never met you, baby, they never met you!

When I returned after the nine-hour drive, I sent Marina this email. I'd been thinking about writing it all the way home.

From: David
To: Marina
Subject: the missing chapters
Sun, 14 Nov 2010 22:08:01 -0600

Marina,

I want to get this to you so I can free my mind of this stuff and explain some of the missing pieces of my life to you.

First, I want to apologize for not being com-passionate enough when you told me numerous times that you were not in a place to start a new relationship. For me to not be persistent or roman-tic is like telling a fish not to swim. The only way I have survived this long in the music business is because of my persistence, especially when it con-cerns something I love. I could never imagine any-thing deeper than the last relationship I was in, but when I hang with you it's even more powerful and profound. I get this euphoric sensation that feels like my car is driving ten feet off the ground when I leave your house.

After nine years of being with a woman who always wanted to feel reassured by connecting five to eight times a day in texts or phone calls, it's taken me some time to get used to how detached you are in that regard. But it's nice to hear your voice once in a while instead of just texting.

One of the things that I had with my ex, and I believe that you and I could have in time, is a spiritual love. This is one of the reasons I'm writing this letter. Emma and I meditated together, did yoga, and went to spiritual retreats together so we could stay connected spiritually, as well as emotionally and physically.

Our love was not nearly that deep in the beginning, but after nine years, I got used to connecting with someone on all those levels. When I moved out in May, a unique thing happened—and it was the last thing that I needed with all of the emotional turmoil and change already going on in my life. A certain part of my body said, "Look, Dave, I know you want to be with another woman right away, but we (your body) are used to having it all—spiritual love, emotional love, and physical enjoyment and since these nice women you are dating are just friends with benefits—this does not satisfy all of the wonderful things that WE (your Body, Mind, and Soul) have gotten used to over the past nine years. So WE (specifically, one part of my body) are not going to work for you right now because it is not fulfilling on any spiritual or emotional level."

I had two incredibly embarrassing situations a month after moving out that were horrifying for a man who had always been very active in that department. So I went to a Zen Buddhist Chinese doctor while I was in Chicago and explained what was going on. He said this didn't make any sense. My pulse was fine and all my organs seemed to be operating normally.

I gave him one of my *Solace* CDs in exchange for his examination and, after looking at the cover, he asked me, "Are you a spiritual man?"

I said, "Yes, I have been meditating for twenty-seven years."

He asked, "Was your wife a spiritual woman?"

I said, "Yes, we used to meditate and do yoga together."

He said, "There's your problem. Your Soul is used to that high spiritual and emotional love. Just having sex with a woman is like taking ten steps down for your Spirit."

I want that high spiritual love again, but this time with someone with whom I can spend the rest of my life.

So my point in telling you all of this is to give you some insight into my process, and why it felt like I was rushing things. I wanted my life and my body to be normal again in every way. And I thought that life had brought us together for a reason.

I met you a few months after I had this real-ization. I guess everyone has a list of qualities that they look for in someone, and the more I spent time with you, the more I felt like you had all of the qualities I was looking for. You are intelligent, spiritual, calm and balanced, athletic, interesting, and you are a yoga instructor which means you are involved in healing. I am a healer with music.

As you have found out, whatever I do, I put 100 percent of myself into it, whether it's music, creativity, or love. I get so much enjoyment from being thoughtful, caring, loving, and affectionate to the special woman in my life. It's not in my nature to just go slow and methodical. I am a passionate artist.

There are things in life we can explain and understand, and there are things that are much more difficult to understand logically.

Try to imagine this: your daughter and your foster child of nine years and your husband disappear and are gone from your life in a flash. You lose your $100,000 down payment on your big beautiful house, and are trying to figure out where you are supposed to go next.

You search around for five months and meet someone who has a daughter that looks very much like the daughter that you just lost, except this daughter does not resist you like one of your previous daughters did. This beautiful new child smiles at you and enjoys you. Every minute you spend with her is like healing salve on a painful wound. Do you get the picture?

It is so easy for me to love Zarina. I wish I could spend more time with her. I want to spend more time with her. If things worked out for us, I would look forward to taking her to the park and kids' movies and shopping, loving her like she's my daughter too, just like I did with Wendy. Then you would have more time to do stuff for yourself.

So when I so wanted to give Zarina a hug goodbye after I played the flutes for her last week, although I am normally very good with words, the words did not come out right because of all the emotions I feel when I spend time with her.

I have to redo my will, and I would like to put Zarina in it. There is a part of me that wants to be everything for her that George would have been for you. How would you ever know these things if I didn't write this to you?

I'm sorry that you have experienced such disappointment over the last couple of years. But isn't it possible that you needed to get that karma out of the way so you could eventually meet me and be far happier than you would have ever been with anyone else?

I'm sure none of them played two flutes for you. And I doubt that any of them wrote music that you listened to twenty times a day.

I've never been so inspired to write so much music for anyone, ever. And I had sworn that I would never write another song for the rest of my life before I met you!

Regarding the bizarre things that happened with our cell phones, losing all of the previous correspondence, it seems like there was some Mercury retrograde activity going on last weekend. I don't think there is a man in this world who wants to share his life with you half as much as I do. And my thought of you coming down for a few days had all the best intentions.

The most difficult thing I am going to ask you is this: try to remember that I adore you and I want to do everything I can to make you happier than you have ever been. Please try to trust me, I won't let you down.

With love,
David

▲ ▲ ▲

To: David
From: Marina
Subject: RE: the missing chapters
Date: Mon, 15 Nov 2010 12:58:34 -0500

David,

Thanks for the lengthy composition offering insight into who you are and where you're coming from. I do admire your persistence when it comes to music—and assertiveness is an undeniably attractive quality, in any capacity. But I feel like when I tell you that I'm not in a receptive place, in terms of being open to a relationship with you, you basically ignore me.

Again, I'm sure your persistence has paid off in music . . . to have reached the level of success you have in your career. Being Grammy-nominated certainly requires a certain tenacity, I'm sure.

That being said, I feel like the more persistent you become, the more I want to distance myself because I feel that we're not on the same page and I'm not effectively communicating with you.

You've certainly been through a lot in your lifetime, as have I . . . and you deserve happiness. I don't want you to waste all of your energy on someone who is not able to be receptive. You have so much to offer the right person . . . and to say you're attentive and generous would be an understatement.

As you know, I think your songs are wonderful. Your gift for singing and songwriting is vastly apparent. I'm honored that I would inspire such creativity, but I feel guilty that you're devoting this time and energy to me when it could be directed at the "right" person.

I completely agree about the emotional, physical, and spiritual connection. The combination is desirable. Without all three—the proverbial ingredients—a relationship might not be sustainable.

Thank you kindly for your invitation to join you and your family for Thanksgiving. That is so nice, since I don't have any family here to share the holiday. But being a vegan and all, I'm kind of grossed out by the whole turkey being sacrificed thing, and Zarina and I (and sometimes a few fellow vegan friends) enjoy a turkey-free day.

I will try to write more soon—I have a webinar coming up in a few minutes and then an appointment, and then have to pick up Zarina . . . possibly I can elaborate and address more later tonight.

Namasté,
Marina

To: Marina
From: David

Thank you for being so clear. You do not need to write more.

David

To David

Sorry if I wasn't more clear before. Is it possible for us to be friends? I'd like it if we could.

Marina,

You were always very clear, but I believe love can heal people.

And as you know, some men love challenges and the chase with women, and I really don't.

Yes, we can be friends, but I can't see you for a while so I can move forward. And I am sure you can understand that.

David

▲ ▲ ▲

David,

I completely understand, of course.

I wish I wasn't in such a wounded, mistrusting place.

Marina

▲ ▲ ▲

To: Marina
From: David

Isn't that the truth! Those two words sum up the whole thing, I've been there, done that, and bought the T-shirt many times over being with someone who had trust issues. I really shouldn't be with someone who has not resolved that because I've already paid my dues in that regard.

You have every reason to have a hard time trusting right now. I imagine Buddha himself could walk into your life and you wouldn't be able to trust him. The sad thing is that both you and I are honest and loyal people. That is why being betrayed, as you have been, hurts so badly. I've been betrayed as well, believe me. If you were not a loyal person, the pain of your disappointment wouldn't have been so bad. It shows, that's the kind of person you are. When I understood how that was one of the things that showed me I could believe in you, I naturally wanted to share life with you because I'm the same way.

As far as the wounded issue, I found out last May, in therapy, that I have chosen women who were wounded because I grew up in a home where my mom was wounded by being in the relationship with my dad. Every significant woman in my life has been deeply wounded. That has been my pattern.

That was something that probably contributed to my falling for you so fast and so deeply.

I also noticed that each time you were getting close to letting me into your heart, you had a knee-jerk reaction to sabotage it because of your fears. I believe it was a defense mechanism you created so you wouldn't get hurt again. You would destroy it so this way you wouldn't give anything a chance to hurt you again. So it became a self-fulfilling prophecy for you. You believe all men will disappoint you now. And even if they aren't disappointing you, your fear and anxiety decides that you better not take a chance on letting that person in—which destroys your chance for love and happiness—which leaves you disappointed. So you're damned if you do, damned if you don't—the result is still the same.

I don't know if I can bring up this next thing without being offensive. I don't mean to be, but what are the chances that your mom projected that same thing onto George after being disappointed in your dad? I don't gamble as a rule, but I would bet on that. That is part of your family history, and you know what they say about history—if we don't learn from it, we repeat it.

How much more similar could your situation be to your mom's? George and I are both men with dark hair and dark eyes. We even look alike! We both do yoga and meditation every day, and sing and play guitar, and write songs with a spiritual message. I never believed in channeling spirits from the other world until now. There have been way too many things happening for me to deny it. A lot of these things I haven't told you about yet, and I'm not sure you would even believe me at this point.

After all of the long life-story emails I've already sent you, who'd think I would have anything left to say?

But I don't want you to feel bad about hurting my feelings. That is not the lesson here. I know I gave you my best. There was nothing more I could say or do to show you what a wonderful man I am, or how much I had to offer you and Zarina. I have to tell you that as loving a mom as you are, you will need a man living with you to properly bring up a child; that's why God set it up this way.

Don't fool yourself into thinking that your child has a dad, and that you don't need any help from a man in your own life. It takes a mom and dad or stepdad living in one house to bring up a kid. I have been there. Once the kid gets to the age of eleven or twelve, they have figured out how to play each parent against each other. This is a ridiculous game these kids become masters at playing.

We choose our destiny by our decisions. I've been trying to stop you from making the mistake of turning your back on real love from a good man, but you couldn't stop yourself. Far more than you have hurt me, you have hurt yourself because you won't allow yourself to love someone who adores you and only wants to make you happy and be a wonderful dad to your child.

That's much sadder than anything I am experiencing, sweetheart.

You can change your destiny, but you won't.

There's a good saying that love and fear cannot occupy the same space, so choose carefully, because that is what you will be left with.

Sincerely,
David

▲ ▲ ▲

To: David
From: Marina

David,

So much of my impression of you and reaction to you were formed in the first week. You know the saying, "You don't get a second chance to make a first impression." You were SO intense, mean, abrupt, and irrational to tell me goodbye because I wouldn't stay up until midnight to greet you home from your travels. And the next day, when we talked through everything, I thought you understood where I was coming from. You acknowledged your poor behavior/reaction. But you then pushed yourself on me as if I never said anything to you. I know I have issues to work through, but you certainly do as well . . . .

Marina

From: David
To: Marina

Of course, I have things to work on. But if you want to see heartless and mean, just text a man after he flies home early to see someone after he gets off the plane and that someone is too tired to see him. Even if it was just for a few minutes to say "Hello" and to give someone a gift because he missed them so much. No one has ever done that to me. And I can only guess if you've ever done that before.

Were you really tired or just afraid? Just think, if you hadn't blown me off, we would have never had that obstacle to deal with the first week.

There are things in life that are not rational, like the feelings I developed for you. There are lots of people who have been married and in love for twenty or thirty years that went through a process when they met their partner. That won't be us.

Love happens, and it is a gift. And you are choosing not to accept it. That's your choice.

I should have never pushed myself on you. That's right, but you couldn't recognize something good in your life even if it was right in front of you and an angel brought it to you on a silver platter.

David

▲ ▲ ▲

To: David
From: Marina

The thing is, David (again, there seems to be such a disconnect within you), you shouldn't have been in such a hurry to see someone who never viewed you as more than a new friend. Then to get so upset . . . it's a wonder I even talked with you after that. I will always be a fan of your music, your voice, and your talent.

I had wanted to remain friends, but honestly, I really see a lot of ego in you and a lot of disconnect. Not saying, again, that I don't have issues to work through, but hopefully this whole ordeal has been a good opportunity for you to do some needed introspective work. I don't think being friends is a great idea at this point.

Marina

▲▲▲

The dragon was victorious. I charged into the studio to record "I Can't Save You from You."

I could save you like the Army
I could save you like the Marines
I could find you in Afghanistan
I could save you in New Orleans
I could save you in New York City
In the barrios of East L.A.
But I can't seem to save you from yourself
No matter what I say
And no matter what I do
I just can't save you from you

I could save you in the desert
If you were burning in the heat
I could warm you from the freezing cold

If you were drowning in the sea
I could save you from a hurricane
That could devastate this town
I could save you if you were buried
Six feet underground
But the only thing I can't do . . .
I just can't save you from you

Chapter 26

Are You Following Me Around?

I drove into town to meet with Gregg, to update him on all of the latest events.

"It's a losing battle," I lamented. "Every time things started going well with her, some gigantic misunderstanding happened. I actually think she's creating these things because she's been so hurt in the past."

"That's sad, bro."

"It's over now," I said, shaking my head. "I really felt that George wanted this to happen because he wanted her to be happy."

Gregg took a deep breath and gave me some advice, "You need to give yourself a rest."

"Do you think I've lost it? Do you think I'm making all this stuff up?"

Gregg hesitated, "Well, I was a Beatles fan, too, but . . ."

"I wasn't a Beatles fan!" I vented with frustration. "I liked them, of course. Who doesn't respect the Beatles? But I don't even know how to play one of their songs! Wait a minute, I did learn "My Sweet Lord" last month . . . but that wasn't even by the Beatles." I started to notice people in the café looking over at us, hearing our heated discussion.

Gregg continued to explain, "All I'm saying is that you need to take it easy for a while and relax. Do something else. Get your mind off Marina."

"I guess you're right. I need to do something. I'm a wreck."

Gregg said, "What you need is some time, yoga, and maybe some Stephanie."

"She's another one I'll never figure out," I pointed out.

After lunch we paid the check and left the restaurant. "Take care . . . and give yourself a break!" Gregg said, heading west down the street.

I walked east up Main Street past an art gallery and a women's boutique. I stopped in a record store featuring collectable vinyl LPs to take a look around. Sitting right on the front counter was an original copy of George Harrison's album, *Cloud Nine*. I turned on my heel and walked out the store, mumbling to myself, *Are you following me around?*

Chapter 27

YouTube Link

From: Marina
To: David
Subject: Daria Lycek shared a link on your
Wall....

David,

Immediately after I sent your email, my girlfriend sent this YouTube link . . . isn't this funny!

Marina

▲▲▲

From: David
To: Marina

When I first saw the YouTube picture in the email, I didn't have my glasses on. I thought it was me, because of the dark hair and dark eyes. You wouldn't have known this, but I only have one 12-string acoustic guitar and it is that guitar. The YouTube triangle was right over the mouth, and since I am usually wearing white when I perform, as you know, I wondered why you were sending me one of my videos. It was only after I put my glasses on that I realized it was George, singing "My Sweet Lord" at *The Concert for Bangladesh*.

You are very good with words, Marina, but maybe there's another word more fitting than "funny."

Your friend's timing of sending you that clip was perfect, as if George sent it to you himself. I've felt that his spirit has been trying to use me to open your heart all along. I did the best I could. I think that is something we can both agree on . . . .

Peace,
David

I forwarded the email to Gregg, who had seriously wondered if I was losing my mind over lunch.

Gregg responded, "Okay, now I'm goose-bumped!"

Chapter 28

10/10/10

10 10 10
I'm not just describing you
It was the day that we met
10 10 10
A day I will always remember
when Life brought you to me
It was actually funny
I never thought I would meet the
girl of my dreams playing football
But after all, it wouldn't matter where I met you
I could see your light shine anywhere
I could see your light shine
I'll remember you always,
With one beautiful tear

10 10 10
Such a special day

It only happens every thousand years
And I'll think back with one beautiful tear,
I never thought I'd meet the girl of my dreams
playing football
But after all, it wouldn't matter where I met you
I would see your light shine anywhere
I could see your light shine anywhere
I could pick you out like a rose in a field of grass
Oh, I could pick you out like a white rose in a
field of grass
So soft, so elegant, so magical yet you can't see
your own magic
I will always remember you with one beautiful tear

10 10 10
If that wasn't love at first sight
Then love doesn't really exist
I only wanted to give to you
And only stole one kiss
I never thought I'd meet the girl of my dreams
playing football
But after all I would have found you anywhere
I could see your light shine anywhere
And I'll remember you every time I see that number
With one beautiful tear, one beautiful tear
If I can only hold the rest of them back
One beautiful tear

▲▲▲

I went into the bathroom to get a tissue and wept, finally accepting that no amount of love or George's energy could help open Marina's heart. Looking in the mirror, I wondered why all of this had even happened. Reminiscing about the whole experience, I wrote "10 10 10."

Twenty-five songs were written and recorded in six weeks describing what it was like to meet someone, start liking them, and eventually love them and their child. Once in a while there was a glimmer of hope, but every time it seemed like they were about to really connect, the legendary venomous dragon reared its ugly head and poisoned it. Eventually, I had to retreat. I thought of how all of these songs told a story, and if I were to give this story a title, I would have called it *Channeling Harrison*.

At that moment, a sense of calm comforted me like a soft breeze, easing my sadness. The thought came that I should write the story, and turn it into a book with a CD of all the songs. This made me feel a little better. My heartache for Marina and Zarina began to ease and slowly I began to feel like myself again. Soon after, I visited my psychic friend Laurie and told her the whole story.

Laurie asked, "So you think you wrote the song 'I'm Still Missing You' for her?"

"Yeah. Why?"

"I don't think that's it at all," Laurie continued. "I think that since George loved her, he still loves her and he wanted her to know that he was still missing her from heaven. He chose you to share the message with her."

"I hadn't looked at it like that."

"And a lot of these songs you've recorded reminded me of Keith Urban," she added.

I said, "I'm not that familiar with his music because I'm a '70s fan, but I saw him on TV in concert a few days ago and he rocks! He's a great guitarist."

▲▲▲

I returned home and wrote this chapter in the book.

"When I met Marina, it was only a few months after I moved away from Wendy, my stepdaughter for nine years, who I loved and missed dearly. My heart was still recovering from that when I met Marina and Zarina. I know how it feels to adopt a child into your heart. As time goes on, it doesn't matter that you weren't there when they were born. I'm sure George wanted to continue being Marina's parent, but after his relationship with her mom ended and they moved back to the States, it wasn't possible.

There are many stories of people who feel they've communicated with their loved ones after they've passed away. Some people believe in life after death, and others don't. Maybe George was looking down from heaven, wanting Marina to know how much he still cared for her and he channeled through me to communicate this to her. Maybe that's why I moved to this town after those strange coincidences with *The Concert for Bangladesh* DVD and the cassette tape in my friend's van. Maybe this was all a set-up. Of all the places I could have landed after my divorce, for some reason I chose this area, just thirty minutes away from where Marina and Zarina lived.

Only two of the Beatles had adopted daughters—George adopted Marina (in his heart, not legally) and Paul adopted Heather. It's strange that I've met each of these daughters at turning points in their lives.

Is it possible that, since Marina lived for a time in England at George's castle, she and Heather may have been playfriends as kids—almost like cousins? From what I've read, the Beatles were like a family. I might be the only person who got to meet both of them as adults.

I met Marina at a critical turning point in her life when she had given up on love. Wouldn't it make sense that George, like every loving parent, wanted her to be happy and find a man worthy of her love who she could finally trust? Someone who shared the experience of missing a stepchild like George did? Someone who meditated, played guitar, and could sing and write spiritual songs for her? I guess I was the best man for the job, and even though it broke my heart, what an honor to be given this charge.

Someday, when my time is over here and I land on the other side of life, where my next chapter will begin, I hope to run into George. I already know what I will say to him: "Thanks for thinking enough of me to pass that message of love to Marina. Now, where do we plug in?"

Chapter 29

Is He an Angel Now?

In spite of my best efforts, I fell into a deep depression. At the deepest depths of my sadness a month later, I had a unique dream. I was sitting on the couch in the house where I lived. The water flooded the room nearly to the ceiling. From the other side of the room, maybe about fifty feet away, a woman with dark hair dove into the water and swam all the way across the room, smiling at me with air bubbles coming out of the corners of her mouth. In her eyes she expressed deep love for me. She swam directly to me and kissed me on the lips. Then she disappeared! She was the same woman with long dark hair that had come into my meditation two months earlier. When I awoke, I was unsure who she might be in real life. My only guess was that it might have been Stephanie from Yogaphoria.

I set a date to go out to dinner with Stephanie again. But it struck me that, though she looked exactly like the woman in the dream, it didn't seem like something she would do. Stephanie and I enjoyed a nice friendship, but she had no romantic interest in me.

Another mystery in my life. I sank back into depression and couldn't get out of bed for days. Karen, my roommate, called Laurie for help. They insisted I shower; then Laurie took me to the mall to get me out of the house for a while.

An African man dressed in a turban and colorful clothing stepped onto the escalator in front of us. Out of the blue he turned to me and said, "You look like a Beatle."

Laurie's jaw dropped. I just stared back at the man.

"Which one?" I asked.

He replied, "You look like you are one of them."

I forced myself to think about something else. "It's getting cold out, and I need a new pair of shoes for winter."

We walked into a shoe store, and I asked Laurie to pick out a pair of boots for me. She chose a pair of dark green suede boots that rose just above the ankle. As we walked on, she saw a grey woolen jacket and said, "That is so you! You have to get that."

Hoping the little shopping spree lifted my spirits. Laurie dropped me off at my house, saying, "Good night. Take care of yourself," and giving me a long hug.

"I'll try."

I went into my bedroom to lie down. There were stacks of papers on my nightstand from all of the songs I'd written, along with CDs of the recordings piled up next to them. My guitar leaned against the wall. I had no desire to play it. Before bed, I sat down to meditate for the first time in weeks.

After a long, deep sigh, I said to myself, "Oh, I need peace. I need some peace." I sang the mantra HU and drifted into my inner sanctum. Fifteen minutes into my meditation, a tingling feeling started to fill my body, beginning in my hands and flows upward into my head. Clarity and calmness gently flowed into my mind.

George appeared in my inner vision, and we stood facing each other. Although he is very serious, a great love flowed through George's eyes as waves of cosmic energy raced through every inch of my body. It felt like I was being spiritually, electrically charged. My body shook and vibrated. That was the last thing I remembered.

▲▲▲

The following morning at the breakfast table, I felt a little better. I told Karen, "George visited me again last night,"

"What did he have to say?" she asked, preparing the morning oatmeal.

"He didn't say anything. He zapped me with this incredible energy. Man, it was powerful."

"So, you're thinking he's some kind of angel now?" she asked.

"I don't know what he is, but he is definitely a lot more than the guitarist from the Beatles. That's for sure. He must have risen to a higher level of consciousness, since he meditated so much when he was alive."

Karen gave me some oatmeal, and we sat down to eat.

"You know," I said, "I really thought the only reason he came to me was because of Marina." I worked on a mouthful of oatmeal, pondered for a moment, then continued, "I guess little Zarina would have been his granddaughter."

"What a darling little girl she is. It was easy to see how much she loved you at the concert."

"I'm really surprised that he's still coming to me. I didn't expect to see him again," I said, dipping my spoon into the oatmeal for another mouthful. Karen made excellent oatmeal.

"Here's something funny I thought of," I said, smiling. "My grandfather's name was Harry, so in the European tradition of family names, my dad would have been a Harryson. So I could have been a Harrison, too."

"You're right!" Karen agreed.

"On a more serious note," I told her, "I think I'm going to move in about a month."

"Where are you thinking of going?" Karen looked worried.

"I haven't decided yet. Maybe Fort Lauderdale. This may sound bizarre, but I feel like someone from my past is looking for me. I don't know exactly what to do about it. I know, however, that I need to make a new start somewhere."

"When do you ever tell me anything that *doesn't* sound bizarre?" she laughed.

"I can't help it. It's my life."

"I'll really miss you," Karen said, placing a hand on my shoulder. "Since you've been here, I haven't needed to watch any of my soap operas. Your life is far more interesting to watch than anything I've ever seen on TV!"

"Thanks, I'm glad you find me entertaining. Maybe you can be my agent," I said with a smile.

After breakfast, I logged onto Facebook. My friend Mike from Long Island sent me a message. "Hey, Dave, hope you're doing well. There's a new group on Facebook called Canarsie from 70th Street to 90th Street that you should check out. I put a posting on there that you changed your name to David Young. Take care, Mike."

Chapter 30

No Direction Calling Me Home

I met with Gregg for lunch up in New Hope. "So Marina never came around?" he asked.

"No. That was the last thing I needed after just going through a divorce five months before I got here. Now I think I know how Van Gogh must have felt," I said.

"Hmmm . . . no word from Stephanie?"

"No, Stephanie and I never really connected."

"Wow, you've been through the ringer," Gregg said, shaking his head.

"I'm taking off soon. Think I'll give it a shot down in Florida. There's nothing working for me here," I reached out to shake Gregg's hand.

"I'm gonna miss you, buddy. Take good care of yourself," Gregg said.

"I'm gonna try." We said goodbye.

I packed up my car and left. The song, "No Direction," played on my car stereo.

I'm looking back, I'm looking forward
I'm looking for something to be heading toward
I've taken a trip and have gone nowhere fast
I'm lost between my future and the past
There's no direction calling me home
No direction calling me home
The only thing I'm sure of is that I'm alone
With no direction calling me home

It isn't easy, I'm finding out
To really know what this is all about
It's hard to be sure, was I right or was I wrong?
Was I following my heart? Did I stay too long?
Now there's no direction calling me home
No direction calling me home
The only thing I'm sure of is that I'm alone
With no direction calling me home

Chapter 31

The Photograph

I called my yoga friend Melanie in Ft. Lauderdale from my cell phone as I drove.

"Is it okay if I come down there and stay with you for a little while? Nothing has worked out for me up here in Pennsylvania."

Melanie said, "Sure, my house is always open to you. The yoga studio that you loved when you were here last time is still two minutes away. That'll be healthy for you."

"Sounds good. I definitely need some healing," I said. "I'll let you know when I get down there. Bye."

Mike called me from Long Island. "Dave, since I posted that you changed your last name to Young, a bunch of old friends from the neighborhood want to get in touch with you. How come you haven't been on Facebook?"

I answered, "I'm in my car driving down to Florida from Pennsylvania. I don't get email on my cell phone. It'll be a couple days until I can get to my computer."

After I hung up, I turned on the radio, and "Layla" came on. Once that song ended, "My Sweet Lord" came on.

I wondered about the connection between the songs, but dismissed it as just a coincidence.

Then Rod Stewart's version of the song "Forever Young," written by Bob Dylan, one of George's closest friends, came on. I felt George's undeniable presence in the car comforting me, filling my heart with the reassuring feeling that it was definitely not just a coincidence.

▲ ▲ ▲

I arrived in Ft. Lauderdale, turned left at George English Park off Sunrise Blvd. and found Melanie's house. She greeted me and invited me to sit with her at the kitchen table. I told Melanie the whole story of what I had just lived through. "You have to finish that book," she said.

"I haven't been able to touch it," I admitted. "It's such a sad chapter of my life."

Melanie lovingly said, "I'll help you. I'm an editor."

"Really? I thought you were a yoga teacher."

With a chuckle, she said, "Yes, I'm that too, but my husband was a well-known writer when he was alive and I edited all of his books and published them. I've edited at least twenty-five books."

"Wow, I had no idea," I said.

"The first thing we need to do is to write a treatment, a three-page synopsis. What are you calling the story?"

"*Channeling Harrison.*"

After lunch, a yoga session, and a shower, I turned on my laptop at a Starbucks. There were quite a few messages in my inbox from excited friends with whom I'd lost touch long ago. The first one was from Danny Behar, who grew up on my street.

"David, long time no see. Mike told me you were headed to Florida. Call me when you get here. I live near Miami."

I called up my old friend and we talked about old times.

Danny hadn't lost his Brooklyn accent. "You won't believe how many people from the old neighborhood live in South Florida. They call it the southern tip of New Yawk."

"I haven't seen or heard from practically anyone after high school. It's been a long time," I said. "Who's down here?"

"Jeffrey Rubin, Bobbie Goldman, Rachel Kingsley . . . ."

"Rachel Kingsley? Oh, my God, I had such a crush on her as a kid," I said. "Wait, someone is beeping in. It's my editor. I gotta go. Let's get together soon."

Melanie was on the other line. "The treatment is done. Why don't you come back and we can go through it together and make any changes you want to it, okay?"

After the review, Melanie said, "If you like, I have a contact who is an agent I work with in Hollywood. His name is Stan Corwin, and he's been in the business a very long time. Would you mind if I sent it to him?"

"Sure, go right ahead."

"Just don't feel bad if he rejects it. He gets so many proposals that he has to turn down nine out of ten things I send him. So don't take it personally if he does."

"Don't worry, I've been in the music business a long time. I can take rejection."

I settled into Melanie's spare bedroom, and finally had time to go online and check my email. Of the many old friends who had contacted me on Facebook by then, one in particular caught my eye.

"David, I have been searching for you for five years. Call me! Rachel Kingsley."

Rachel lived one street down from me on East 83rd Street in Brooklyn. We went to the same schools, and played in band together. We kissed one time at a spin-the-bottle party in sixth grade; but shortly after, it was her turn to kiss my best friend, Barry Yagoda. Barry asked her out, not knowing that I had a giant crush on her. When I entered junior high school, most of the girls wanted to date older boys—and from that time through high school, I was secretly in love with Rachel. I didn't have a girlfriend most of those years because of my feelings for her, and I never went to my prom.

"What happened to you after high school?" I asked. "I heard you moved to South America and graduated early."

"I did," she said. "My parents were from Columbia and since I went there on summer vacation every year, I met a man there and got married right out of high school. I have two kids and they're all grown up now."

"Was it an arranged marriage? We all thought it was."

"No, not at all. My parents actually didn't want me to marry so young."

Rachel and I made plans to meet with Danny and his wife at Hollywood Beach for dinner. I felt very distant and moody when I arrived. As we walked along the boardwalk to a restaurant that Danny had picked out, I pointed to a lighted vessel off in the distance. "I wonder whether that's a cruise ship or a cargo ship,"

Rachel responded, "I'm not sure."

I don't know why, but I blurted, "That's not the only thing you weren't sure of."

Danny and his wife looked at each other, wondering what kind of evening they had ahead of them.

After we were seated at the restaurant and ordered, Rachel attempted to make conversation.

"I went to your website. I can't believe how many CDs you've made. What do you like to do, besides music?"

"I enjoy doing yoga."

"Really? I enjoy yoga as well." She added, "I also like to paint."

"I've never painted anything."

"You should try it sometime," Rachel replied. "It's very therapeutic. Speaking of therapeutic, I have something to show you."

Rachel pulled a picture out of her purse. It was an old Polaroid of the two of us kissing at the party thirty-five years ago at Gary's house in sixth grade.

I was speechless, and looked at the photo for five minutes without saying a word.

"There weren't any cell phones or digital cameras back in those days. Where did you get this?" I asked, still stunned.

Rachel answered, "I have no idea who took the photo or how it got to me, but I've had it in the bottom of a box all these years. When I got divorced five years ago and Face-book came out, I started looking for you. But since you had changed your last name, I couldn't find you. No one knew what happened to you."

"Really?"

"Really. I had a crush on you the whole time in school. Even before we kissed that one time in sixth grade at Gary's party, I always thought you were the cutest, and never understood why you didn't ask me to go steady."

"You've got to be kidding me. This is the biggest misunderstanding since Adam and Eve!" I said in amazement.

I showed Danny's wife Maria the photo, and she began to cry. She said something to Danny in Spanish.

I asked Danny, "What did she say?"

"She loves novels," Danny answered, "and this is the most romantic story she's ever heard."

Danny handed her a tissue.

I asked Rachel, "Where do you live now?"

"About half-an-hour from Fort Lauderdale in Aventura."

Danny chimed in. "I hear there are some pretty famous people who live in Aventura, right on that circle of condos."

Rachel added, "I live on that circle!" She gave Danny a big smile.

"Do have any hobbies? What else do you like to do?" I asked.

"Since my grandparents lived by the ocean in Columbia, I always loved swimming," Rachel said, with her incredible smile.

At that moment, I realized that Rachel was the woman who swam to me in the dream where my house was flooded a month ago. She was the woman with brown hair that flew into my meditation, kissed me on the lips and disappeared.

She looked so much like Stephanie from Yogaphoria, they could have been sisters. By the end of the night, it felt as if we'd been together for years. We said goodbye to Danny and Maria, and went for a walk down the beach.

Rachel asked, "What's up with the Beatle boots and the Beatle jacket?"

"You're right. They do look like Beatle boots. I never realized that."

I told her everything that happened and she was very uncomfortable hearing it, wondering if I still had feelings for Marina. The story was also so far-fetched, it sounded like I might be crazy.

A few days later, we met at Rachel's house. She showed me some of her paintings. One of them, a two-tone grey painting with six unfinished triangles caught my eye.

"Why haven't you finished that one?" I asked.

"I don't know. Do you want to paint this with me? It's easy."

"No, some other time maybe," I replied. "It would be fun to do something together with that one someday."

Then I asked, "What type of work do you do?"

Rachel answered, "I'm a graphic artist and I do catalogs for an international distribution company in Hollywood, Florida. My office is right off Young Circle on Harrison Street."

Chapter 32

The Painting and the Rolling Stone

Acouple months later, Rachel and I moved in together. Melanie called me with good news, "I just heard back from Stan. He read the synopsis for *Channeling Harrison* and liked it. He wants to meet with you."

"Okay, I'll book a flight to Los Angeles. Sounds good!"

I shared this news with Rachel, and we celebrated the possibility. After dinner we stopped at Bed, Bath and Beyond to look around. I spotted a painting with seven burgundy trees painted on a gold, grey, and brown background. "We have to buy this one for the bedroom," I said.

"But there's a three-inch crack in the canvas," Rachel said.

"I know. I saw it, but I really like this painting."

"Are you crazy? Who buys a new painting with a giant defect in it!"

"I'm not leaving here without it!" I said adamantly. Rachel thought I was completely nuts!

We found the store manager and Rachel bargained the price down to $69, with the understanding that they order another one and call us when it arrived.

We brought it home and hung it above our bed. Then, looking around, it struck me. "We need something for this other wall. Could we take the grey painting that you never finished and add these colors to it so it matches the one with the burgundy trees that we just bought?"

"Sure, we can paint it together," Rachel said. "It'll be fun."

We spent two hours adding burgundy, gold, and brown to the grey painting. Rachel cleaned up the brushes and I hung it up.

When we sat down on the bed and looked at it, I remarked, "We should add more shapes with the same colors to it."

Rachel said, "Fine, I don't care if we get rid of all of the grey."

We painted for another hour, making more geometric figures out of the triangles. Rachel cleaned up the brushes and I re-hung it.

After a few minutes of looking at it, again, I said, "I still don't think it's finished. I need to take it down again."

I drove Rachel crazy for ten hours, putting it up and taking it down, adding more color, and then her cleaning up the brushes.

At 10:30 p.m., she was exasperated. "You can paint all you want, but I'm not cleaning up the brushes one more time. If you want to do any more painting, you can clean up the brushes. I can't believe what a perfectionist you are. You just don't quit!"

"I can't stop until I feel like it's done. And it's just not done yet." Again, I pulled the painting down, adding more paint and more shapes and triangles.

I cleaned the brushes and then hung it up again. Rachel was exhausted and was in bed by then. I took it down one more time.

She said, "I don't know what drives you like this."

"This is how I do everything I do," I explained, "Just ask the engineers who have been recording my music."

Finally, I was at peace with the painting. It looked great on the wall next to the picture bought from Bed, Bath and Beyond. We fell asleep, exhausted.

That night I had a dream and woke Rachel to tell her about it.

"George came to me again last night. He was playing hide and seek in a recording studio with me and when I finally caught up with him, he said, 'I like to play tennis with soft grass behind me.'

"I didn't understand what he meant and asked, 'What?'

"Trying to hold back his smile, he repeated, 'I like to play tennis on soft grass.' Then he burst out laughing and disappeared.

"He was happy and joking around with me, not so intense like my other experiences with him. Why would he tell me that? I didn't know you could even play tennis on grass. Isn't that bizarre?"

"Yes, it is," Rachel said. "Can we go back to sleep now?"

A few days later, Rachel brought home a gift for me, a special issue of *Life* magazine called "Remembering George Harrison."

As I paged through the pictures, I came across a photograph of George and Ravi Shankar, his close friend and sitar teacher, who also played at The Concert for Bangladesh. The photo was taken backstage after the performance.

George wore a jacket with a unique design of triangles and geometric shapes in burgundy, gold, and brown with a little bit of light grey in the pattern. *It was the exact pattern and colors of my first painting.*

The following week, Rachel dropped me off at the Ft. Lauderdale Airport to fly to Los Angeles to meet Stan Corwin about my book proposal. While walking to the gate, I passed a magazine shop and saw George Harrison on the cover of the September issue of *Rolling Stone* magazine. I bought it and sat down to read, waiting to board the plane. As I paged through the article, there was a picture of George playing tennis with the grass behind him!

Forever Young

Harrison and Bob Dylan, playing tennis on the Isle of Wight in 1969. To Harrison, Dylan was both a friend and hero. "George used to hang over the balcony videoing Bob while Bob wasn't...

He was having a blast, playing tennis with Bob Dylan in a grassy area!

Under the photo were the words "Forever Young" in bold. Only my closest friends have called me David "Forever" Young.

There were numerous things in the interview with George's wife, Olivia, that had never been talked about in public, that I had experienced the previous year—the most profound thing being that, at the exact moment when George passed away, Olivia said "the room was filled with a glowing light that lit up the room."

That is the way I described the light I saw in the studio while recording the song "I'm Still Missing You" for Marina.

I boarded the plane deep in thought, wondering, *Why is he lining up one thing after another in my life?*

▲ ▲ ▲

I became so obsessed with the world of color that hardly anything else mattered. I'd wake up at 4:00 a.m. and paint until 7:30, when Rachel got up for work. I'd stop only because she insisted that I stop painting for a half-hour to talk to her.

After she'd leave, I would paint non-stop until 6:30 p.m. when she returned and prepared dinner. She was very impressed by the progress I was making as a new painter, but was growing more and more frustrated feeling like she was losing me to my passion.

After dinner, I'd immediately start painting again until 1:00 or 2:00 a.m. and then sleep until 4:00. This went on for months.

I only took a break during the day to do hot yoga. My friends owned the Yoga College of India in Ft. Lauderdale, a loving, supportive studio five minutes from the beach where they offer eight classes a day with thirty to sixty students in each. The classes were ninety minutes in a temperature of ninety-five-degrees, and I attended three or four times a week. I became a lean, spiritual, musical painting machine.

The Om symbol is a recognized logo at most yoga studios. It is the sound of one of the heavenly spiritual planes that many sing as a mantra in meditation. It represents peace.

I decided to paint an Om, so I bought a large 3' x 4' canvas. Under the symbol I wrote in cinnamon, "All You Need Is Love." Eventually a large wave of crimson, burnt orange, blues, sparkling yellows, and indigo flowed out of the center, and mostly covered the cinnamon letters.

I blended the acrylic paint with basil to thicken it, which created a rich texture about 1/4" thick. Don't ask me why I added basil to it. I didn't know that the Hindu monks did this when they made their mandalas.

For two weeks, I lived in the world of this painting. Anything else felt like an annoyance and an unwelcome distraction.

It's been so long since you've been away
I still have this feeling that doesn't go away
We can't live together, we can't be apart
Living without you is tearing me apart

But I've got this restless heart, this restless heart
I've got this restless heart, it doesn't go away

My good friend Dan says I should settle down
He said, "Stop making life so complicated,
And quit messing around!"

But I've got this restless heart, this restless heart
I've got this restless heart, it doesn't go away

On weekends I performed at art festivals, colorful out-door venues surrounding me, and my new appreciation for art made playing music almost secondary in my life. I still spent most of the day playing my flutes and selling CDs, but my mind was focused on learning about art and the use of color. I soaked up all I could, surrounded by the paintings of the great painters who exhibited at the shows.

One of my friends thought I was onto something, and suggested that I bring my artwork to the festivals to show them. I appreciated the compliment and started to bring them along. Although I felt like I was just a beginner, I sold one the first weekend I brought them!

The art festival circuit in South Florida is a vibrant scene. Every weekend, in just about every town, the streets fill with artists of all types. Locals and snowbirds alike flock to gawk, admire, and purchase the rainbows of possibilities.

My art, with its spiritual overtones, attracted a select group of admirers, especially since spirituality has become so popular in recent years. At times, my music almost seemed inconsequential as my art pulled for the attention of the pass-ers-by. This was a unique experience for me, to say the least.

One weekend, after awakening from a unique dream, I saw a picture of Emma in my mind's eye. This dream was more of a waking, spiritual experience, like a movie playing.

She and her new boyfriend were standing together smiling, while the song "Let It Be" played in my mind. It was surreal. It had been about a year since Emma and I made our final attempt at saving our nine-year relationship. There'd been so much drama and trauma over the past months, a peace had finally come into my heart regarding her. I sincerely wanted her to be happy. Though I missed the fun and passion we once shared, I wasn't looking back anymore. Painting filled the space that women previously held in my life, at least for the moment.

I lay in bed, taking in the dream. The song that spirit supplied was obvious direction and symbology—let Emma be in peace.

I hadn't been thinking about her, and wondered what spurred on the dream. I had finally let her go. I texted her the details of the dream, ending the message with, "I truly wish you all the happiness in the world."

I arrived at the art show at 9:00 a.m. to finish setup. My booth was deep in the show, so it would probably be another hour or so until customers started showing up in my area.

At 10:00 a.m. my cell phone rang. It was Emma. Her voice was weak and she was sniffling.

"Do you have a cold?"

"No," she replied.

"Then what's wrong?"

"I got your text message. And I want to tell you some things." Her voice was breaking up with emotion.

"Okay."

"The happiest days of my life were with you. I've never loved anyone in my life as much as I loved you. You were so good to Wendy and Mandy. I know we can't be together in this life. I just loved you too much, and it made me crazy thinking about losing you.

"You were like my heroin. I was addicted to you and to the incredible passion we had together. I love Jed and he is *sooo* good to me. We have a beautiful relationship that has stability, but he's not you and I'm convinced that I'm never going to love him as deeply and passionately as I loved you. But I know we can't go back."

"I know we can't go back, too. Those years were also the best years of *my* life. If I added up all the happiness I had with every woman in my life, it wouldn't equal the happiness I had with you."

I remained calm, and avoided getting caught up in the emotion that Emma poured out until she said, "I want to spend eternity in heaven with you!" Sobbing, she continued, "Then I want to reincarnate with you and have your children and enjoy every second of life with you! I miss you so bad it's hard to breathe sometimes. But I know I can't go through any more heartache with you." She burst out crying and then hung up the phone.

I was okay before Emma's call, but now it was all I could do to hold back my own torrent of tears. *How am I going to work? How can I even think about standing in my booth five more minutes, let alone seven more hours?* A giant ball of emotion lodged in my throat.

The woman in the booth across from me saw this and came over to me.

"Oh, my God. What happened to you? Who were you on the phone with?"

It was obvious that I was about to burst into tears.

"That was the woman I spent nine of the best years of my life with. I adopted her kids, we bought a house together that we had to give back to the bank last year. And she just told me . . . ."

A young man in his thirties walked up, the first customer of the day. The woman left and walked back to her booth across the aisle.

I wasn't sure I could speak, so I stayed silent, waiting for the customer to ask a question. The man looked around at all of my art hanging in the booth, sometimes looking up close at some of the pieces to study the details.

Five minutes passed. Then he turns to me and bluntly says, "These paintings look like something George Harrison would have painted."

I was in shock. "Why would you say that?"

The young man nonchalantly responded, "I don't know, they just remind me of him."

"But you weren't even born when the Beatles were around," I responded.

The man left the booth. I was so stunned by his remark that I forgot all about the conversation with Emma.

Rachel and I had flown to New Jersey to visit my family for Thanksgiving.

I was in such a terrible place. I wasn't *close* to the edge anymore—I was *on* the edge. I couldn't take the pain I was living with inside me.

I had a dream. In my dream, my grandma was in a group of about six other people—her brothers and sisters, who were my great aunts and uncles, and who I didn't really remember. Mom's baby sister, Nancy, was standing off a few feet to the right from them. I did remember that my Aunt Nancy, who died young, adored the Beatles. My grandmother looked over, saw me and started to walk towards me. She was the kindest, most loving person in the world. She was the perfect example of love and goodness, but she had the most serious look on her face—a look I had never seen. Her eyes bore into my soul like a giant drill and she told me, "Don't you even think of taking your life! Do you know what that would do to your mother!"

I started crying in the dream, and even woke up crying.

Over the next few days, any thought of it brought me to tears. I was a mess that week during the family visit.

When Rachel and I returned to Florida, we decided to get lunch at the hotel where we had parked the car because I was hungry. The restaurant was called The Rickenbacker. This made me smile because George had made the 12-string Rickenbacker electric guitar famous. That was the guitar he played to create the jangly sound in the beginning of the Beatles' songs "A Hard Day's Night" and "Ticket to Ride." After that, bands like The Byrds used it and it became a prominent sound of the middle part of the 1960s.

After lunch when we returned to the apartment, I had a really strong urge directing me to look at the book on George's life that Rachel had given me just before we left on the trip. I'd left it on the coffee table and hadn't read it yet. As I paged through it, about halfway in, I came upon the picture of George wearing his favorite jacket at the after-party of The Concert for Bangladesh. *It was the same design, and the same exact colors.*

Over the following days, I came to realize that the real reason I had reconnected with Rachel was because without her, her paints, and that grey painting with the six triangles, I would have never, ever thought of painting. I believe that George wanted me to paint because he wanted to give me proof—evidence that what I was experiencing and trying to communicate to people was *true.*

In a few more months, though, I also realized that I couldn't live with Rachel any longer. I moved out, though we remained friends.

Chapter 33

Layla

I temporarily moved back to Cliffside Park, New Jersey to stay at my mom's place. This coincided with the New York City Spa Convention at the Javitts Center, where I'd purchased a booth to sell my spa music.

We were having lunch at my mom's apartment, when out of the blue she asks, "Why don't you try to connect with Heather McCartney?"

I almost choked on my tuna fish sandwich. "What? Where did that come from?"

"There was a story in the *New York Times* this week on her sister Stella, who is a designer, so I thought of her . . . you're single now." Mom gave me the look, "Why not?" and then added, "She's blonde . . . and she liked your music at the event that Paul came to in Atlanta."

It was a good idea. I was married at the time of that event. When Heather walked in the room, I definitely felt something between the two of us, but my mind was struggling to take in everything that was happening with Paul's friendly approach. I thought she was beautiful, though. I told my mom that twelve years ago, and somehow she remembered.

"I have to get my stuff ready for the show," I said, finishing my lunch. "Can't believe you just said that to me."

New York is known for its large Italian/Jewish population, who are usually dark-haired, dark-eyed people. Not many blondes with blue eyes—unfortunately.

Halfway through the first day of the show, a gorgeous blonde with blue eyes walked up to my booth while I was talking with another customer about relaxing music for spa treatment rooms. I couldn't help but notice her. She patiently waited her turn for me to finish talking with my customer, checking me out hard from the side of my corner booth.

I walked over to her.

"Thanks for waiting. My apologies. This show has been really busy, much better than last year, and I didn't bring enough help this time. How are you?"

"I'm fine," she said. "Wow, your music is *sooo* peaceful."

"Thanks. I've been doing these spa shows all over the country for many years, and I've sold music to over 10,000 spas and massage therapists."

"Well, I can definitely see why."

"Are you a massage therapist or an esthetician?" I asked.

"I'm an esthetician."

"Where is your spa?"

"I don't work out of a spa. I do skincare out of my home."

"What part of the city is that?"

"Edgewater."

"Edgewater, New Jersey? Right next to Cliffside Park?"

"Yeah, why do you ask?"

"Because I just moved into an apartment in Cliffside Park yesterday. What a small world . . . and you're blonde."

She looked at me strangely, "Well yeah . . . ."

"Would you like to join me for dinner tomorrow night?"

"Sure, I'd like that. Here's my card."

I looked closely at her card and discovered two things. First, her name was Renee. Second, the picture on it distinctly reminded me of the *Layla* album cover that Eric Clapton made with Derek and the Dominoes.

"Layla," I said to myself.

"What did you say?"

"Nothing. I'll see you tomorrow night."

The following night, I picked her up at her stylish apartment overlooking Manhattan.

"You're place is like five minutes from me, and my apartment practically looks down at your building. If that building wasn't in the way, and the road wasn't so winding, I could look out my window and see you."

"Isn't that a coincidence?!"

"My life seems to be one never-ending coincidence."

"What do you mean?"

"Long story," I laughed. "Very long story."

We enjoyed sushi at a restaurant looking out over the city. I was attracted by her beauty, but after the roller coaster ride I'd just been on with Marina, I definitely moved slower than I had in the past.

"So where did you grow up?" I asked.

"Actually, not too far from here in Clifton."

"And you're actually blonde?"

"What's up with the blonde thing?"

Laughing at myself, I explained, "Well, the happiest days of my life were with someone with blonde hair and blue eyes. Gold and blue are my two favorite colors. When I came back to New York, I didn't think I'd ever meet anyone here with blonde hair because everyone's Italian or Jewish and you're just so . . . exactly what I'm attracted to."

"Well that's nice of you to say."

It was hard for me to believe that something could be going so right after all so many ups and downs.

After dinner, I dropped her off at her apartment and said, "That was nice. Would you like to try this again?"

"Sure, I'm working tomorrow night, but I'm free Wednesday."

"Okay. Great."

Wednesday night finally arrived, and when I picked her up, she looked even more beautiful than the first night. We went out for Indian food, and I felt my heart opening. We had a wonderful time.

I drove her home after dinner and as we sat in my car, I debated whether to just kiss her good night or ask her first. (Marina definitely didn't want to be kissed, and that image kept going through my mind.)

After an agonizing amount of small talk, I finally blurted, "Is it okay if I kiss you good night?"

Disappointed, she answered, "That was your first mistake. You should have just kissed me."

I felt like I'd just blown the vibe from thinking too much. I leaned over to kiss her and, because it's quite a stretch in my SUV, I twisted my neck and yelled, "Ouch!"

"What was that?" she asked.

"I just twisted my neck," I said, as I tried to massage some of the kinks and cramping.

"Well, I hope to see you soon."

A few days later, we went out for a walk by the Hudson River. It curved around the back of a shopping mall and afforded us a nice view of the Manhattan skyline.

Renee said, "My shoulder has been killing me after I fell in a bizarre bike accident, and I have to have surgery next week."

"Well, that stinks."

"I haven't slept well in months."

"That must be going around," I sympathized. "I don't know anyone who sleeps well anymore."

We stopped at a café and I ordered a glass of red wine. The waiter brought me a giant glass of merlot.

"I hardly ever drink," I said. "Actually, I didn't have a drink for twenty-seven years, but now that I'm single again and dating, I really enjoy a nice glass of red wine."

She added, "I wish I could have one of those, but I'm on antibiotics and I can't."

The wine was beginning to affect me. I felt a little lightheaded with a buzz.

"You know I've wanted to tell you something since you gave me your card at the show. Your picture on the card really reminds me of the cover of the *Layla* album. Do you remember that one?"

"No, I don't remember it at all. Who made it?"

"Eric Clapton had a band with Duane Allman called Derek and the Dominoes. There's a really cool story about it."

"Really? Tell me."

"Well, from what I remember, Eric and George Harrison were best friends. Eric fell in love with George's wife, Pattie. It messed him up so badly, it drove him to heroin addiction. That's why he wrote the song "Layla." You know, 'You got me on my knees, Layla.'"

"Wow, but didn't he marry her?"

"Yes, after George and Pattie split up. And then he wrote, 'Wonderful Tonight' for her.

"Oh, that's so romantic."

"Some women just pull the songs right out of you."

"Let's look up the CD on Google so I can see what it looks like."

She typed it into her phone. I did not have a good feeling about this.

"You think I look like *her*?" Renee gave me a dirty look. (She's a model and very self-conscious about her appearance.)

"Well, the hair on your business card curls up on the sides. It reminded me of the way hers curls up."

That definitely blew the vibe between us. The date ended shortly thereafter. No good-night kiss.

The following weekend, I flew to Montreal for another spa show, and while in my hotel room I decided to logon to Facebook to kill some time. I looked up Renee and browsed through her profile pictures, saw we had one mutual friend. Hmmm . . . who could that be?

"OMG, there's no way!" I said aloud. Our mutual friend was Marina!

God. *This is terrible*, was my next thought.

The more I thought about Marina and Renee being friends, the more paranoid I got. *Are they close friends or just acquaintances?* I wondered. What if Renee had realized we had a mutual Facebook friend, and had contacted Marina already? Had Marina told her that she thought I was an obsessed nut job who couldn't get over her?

The following day, I sent Marina a text message: "Hi there. I hope you are well. I need to talk with you." I hadn't contacted her in quite a while and wondered if she would even respond.

Marina texted back, "Call me at nine-thirty tonight. That's when Zarina goes to bed. Nice to hear from you."

I called her, "Hi. How are you?"

"Fine. Much better, thanks. How have you been?"

"It's been up and down, but I'm okay," I said. "I need to ask you something."

"What's up?"

"I know we were friends and we wanted to try to stay friends, and at the end there were some intense words between us."

"Yeah. And where are you going with this?" she said as kindly as she was able.

"Well, after I moved back to New York I met someone, and we started dating and I liked her. It wasn't intense like when I met you, but she was nice. Then she just cut it off and I wasn't sure why. I just flew to Montreal and had some time to kill in my hotel room, so I went on Facebook and looked her up. I discovered that she and I had a mutual friend. You!"

"Oh, my gosh! Who is it?"

"Renee Booth."

"Yes, I know Renee. She's a sweetheart. We bumped into each other occasionally at different modeling jobs and became friends. Not close friends, but friends. Why? What happened?"

"I'm not completely sure. We went out a few times and I made a little comment about something that wasn't a big deal, and she just totally disconnected. When I looked her up on Facebook and found out about the mutual friend thing, I wondered if she saw that and contacted you. And so I wondered since we had left off on such a sour note if you had told her that I was . . . well . . . crazy or something."

Marina surprised me with her response. She said, very sincerely, "I wouldn't say anything bad about you. Actually, I wanted to thank you."

"Thank me? For what?"

"When I met you I was in such a bad place, as I'm sure you remember. My confidence and self-esteem were gone. I felt terrible about myself.

"So when you came along and were *sooo* persistent and didn't give up on me, and wrote all of those beautiful songs for me, it made me think maybe I still had some good qualities that I just couldn't see. If you saw something good in me and were the respectable man that you are, then maybe I wasn't as bad as I thought.

"That gave me a renewed confidence in myself again, and a few months later I met a good man who I cared for, who also cared for me. Now we're together, in love, and adopting a son together. So I'm glad that you called so I could thank you for not giving up on me."

I was almost speechless, but persisted anyway, "So you didn't say anything bad about me to Renee?"

"Of course not."

"Well, that is so nice to hear. All of it."

"I'm getting tired because our little one has been keeping us up. If you're ever in the area, let me know."

"Okay, I will. Good night."

"Good night, David."

Chapter 34

The Beatles and the Bard

The foreclosure of my house in Minneapolis was imminent and Emma called me to tell me the sad news. After some heated words, I asked her to tell Wendy that I loved her and missed her. Emma sharply replied, "You're just a bard in her life."

This was not a word I had ever heard Emma use and was actually shocked to hear it come out of her. Plus, I didn't even know what a bard was!

I was in Las Vegas exhibiting at a spa conference and was staying at my friend Vicky's house. I needed to ask Jeff, my business manager at my office a few questions so I called him up. He could tell there was something wrong right away.

"What's up? You don't sound good."

"Emma and I just spoke and at the end of our conversation she called me a bard. She said I'm just a bard in Wendy's life."

"What is a bard?" Jeff asked.

"I'm not sure, but it can't be good."

Jeff looked it up on Google. "It says that a bard is a poet or a traveling storyteller. Oh, and Shakespeare was called The Bard."

"Well I'm sure she didn't mean it as a compliment."

Laughing, Jeff said, "Yeah, I'm sure not. Feel better, I have to go. Someone's on the other line."

I sat there on the bed and felt prompted to look over at the nightstand on the right side of my bed. Surprised, I saw a Beatles book there. A photographer of the band had found a box of film from the early years that had never been seen. As I paged through it, a chapter jumped out at me, The Beatles and The Bard, with a picture of George underneath it, dressed up, doing Shakespeare.

Chapter 35

12/12/12

Six months later, after many road trips, I arrived back in New York. It was December 16, 2012. While driving to my apartment, I scanned the radio to find something different to listen to, and came across a smaller station playing Indian sitar music. After the piece ended, the DJ sadly announced, "Our beloved friend Ravi Shankar, the master musician, passed away last week on 12/12/12. He left us a legacy of music that we will treasure forever. A concert celebrating his life will be held on Monday night, December 17th at the Academy in Brooklyn from 9:00 p.m. until 9:00 a.m. Please join us. All are invited."

I knew I had to go. I thought it odd that I met Marina on 10/10/10, and Ravi Shankar passed on 12/12/12.

The next morning I sent out this text to every person I knew in New York and New Jersey. And just for the hell of it, I included Renee.

"Hi everyone. I just got back from the road and there is a benefit concert for Ravi Shankar tonight in Brooklyn. Does anyone want to join me?"

The first person who texted back was Renee. I hadn't spoken with her in nine months.

"Hi, David. I would have loved to join you, but I have to work tonight. Have fun. Let's get together soon."

That was a surprise.

It was strange. Hardly any of my friends responded at all. After a late afternoon business meeting in Manhattan, around quarter past seven, I checked my phone and there were texts from each of my two closest friends, Carlos and Scott.

Carlos wrote, "Yo, Dave. Que pasa? Good to have you back in New York. The concert sounds awesome, but I'm playing a gig at the Copacabana on 46th Street at seven-thirty. Why don't you stop by before the concert?"

Scott wrote, "David Forever Young. How are you, my brother? Can't make the concert tonight. There's a party at eight-thirty at my friend Harry's apartment on 77th and Columbus uptown. I told him I would play. Why don't you stop by there before you head over to Brooklyn? There's gonna be nice people there."

I stood at the corner of 34th Street and 7th Avenue wondering which way to go. Since the concert would be going until 9:00 a.m. the following morning, I decided to walk over to the Copa to see Carlos and then see Scott uptown.

When I arrived at the Copa, the band was still setting up onstage and the club was preparing for a special event taking place. Apparently, a singles website called the Golddiggers

Club was hosting a mixer and there were booths around the perimeter populated by different businesses wanting to reach the thirty-ish single woman and fifty-sixty-ish single, successful businessman demographics.

I walked up to the stage and Carlos saw me. That night, Carlos was playing flamenco guitar in a Latin band.

"Hey, bro! So good to see you," Carlos said, with his biggest smile.

"Same here. What's goin' on here?"

"We're doing this corporate event and are running late."

I commented, "This has to be the cheesiest meet-up group I've ever seen."

"I know, right?"

I looked around the club, scanning the different booths around the perimeter of the dance floor from the left side of the stage all the way around the bar and back to the right side. The booth closest to the band was an anti-aging skincare business with a cute blonde standing there, talking to a potential customer. When the customer left, the blonde turned and my jaw dropped in disbelief. *Renee!*

"Oh, my God," I said to Carlos, "you are not going to believe this! I know that woman! I dated her nine months ago, and when I told her she reminded me of the woman on the cover of the *Layla* album, she got pissed at me and never went out with me again. I texted her this morning and asked her to go to the Ravi Shankar concert tonight. She said she would have loved to go, but she had to work. That's unreal."

Carlos said, "She's a babe! I need to finish setting up. We're running late."

"I think I'll go say Hi to her, then go see my friend Scott uptown. I'll come back later."

I stepped down off the stage and headed toward Renee's booth. As I approached, Renee made eye contact with me, staring in disbelief.

"What are *you* doing here?" I asked.

"This is where I'm working tonight. I'm a spokesperson for this laser and skin-care company. What are you doing here?"

"My good friend Carlos plays in the band hired to play tonight. I've never been here before. What a small world. I can't believe you're here!"

"I told you I had to work tonight."

"Do you do a lot of events here?"

"No, I've never been here either."

Recognition of this amazing coincidence struck us both at once.

Renee asked, "Are you here for this cheese ball event?"

"No way! I just came by to say Hi to Carlos. I'm headed to a party uptown. I'll be back later. What time are you here 'til?"

"Midnight."

"Okay. I'll be back before then."

"Sounds great. I'll see you later, then."

"Definitely."

I walked away, but caught Carlos' eye, who smiled with a big "thumbs up" as I left the club.

Out on the street, I hailed a taxi and headed uptown to visit Scott at his party. The building was a four-story walkup in a classy brownstone. When I arrived, the door was open and about ten people in their forties were sitting around the living room drinking red wine. Scott sat in a chair playing guitar in front of the two puffy couches where they all sat.

Scott Paige is a handsome, semi-hippie with medium length hair, a light-brown beard, and a warm friendly demeanor. He stopped playing his beat-up acoustic guitar and with his witty, loveable sense of humor said, "Ladies and gentlemen, please let me introduce you to my good friend, the one and only, Mr. David Forever Young."

Everyone smiled and clapped a little, playing along with Scott's playfulness.

I said, "On behalf of the band and myself, I hope we pass the audition."

Everyone laughed and lifted up their glasses.

"You don't have to tell me all your names. I'll never remember them all, anyway."

Scott said, "David's the guy who plays two flutes at one time and sold over a million CDs of spiritual music.

"And this is Harry. I was apartment sitting here for him, and he just got back from San Francisco. This is his welcome back party."

"Nice to meet you, Harry," I said, reaching out my hand.

"A pleasure. Nice to have you here at our little soirée."

I couldn't help checking out the women at the party as I sipped a little red wine. Scott started to play another acoustic song, and I turned my attention from the couch to him. At first I watched his hands and fingers strum the guitar. As I lifted my eyes to watch Scott sing, I saw a painting above Scott's head. A painting of the *Layla* album cover!

I asked Harry, "Where did that painting come from?"

"I painted it myself thirty years ago when I was in high school," Harry replied.

Another coincidence beyond imagination in my life.

I went off into a daze. I was awakened from my dream by the clapping of Scott's friends at the end of his last song.

Scott stood up, took a comical bow, and sat down next to me.

"So how are you doing, bro?"

"Amazing."

"Ahh. The amazing flute man and his amazing stories. Has George planted any more seeds in your life lately?"

I was sipping my wine and almost choked up my last swallow.

"Scott, I've told you all the things that have happened. And every time I think they're done, something more incredible happens. It's hard to believe. I don't know what he's trying to tell me or why he keeps planting these things in my life. I'd like to tell you how crazy this Layla painting is, but I have to get back to the Copacabana soon."

Scott called over to his friend, finishing his beer, "Hey, Harrison, I need another one of these."

In disbelief, I asked Scott, "Why did you just call him Harrison?"

"'Cuz that's his nickname. We all call him Harrison."

"Oh, my God, there really never is a dull moment in my life."

I snapped a picture of the *Layla* painting on my cell phone.

"I thought you were going to the concert for Ravi Shankar in Brooklyn," Scott said.

"Well I was, and I still might later, but first I have to go back and see Layla—I mean, Renee."

"All right. Well, take care." Scott gave me a bear hug. "Let's get together soon."

"You got it, bro."

I hailed a cab to take me back downtown to the Copacabana. The exciting lights, colors, and energy of the city flashed by the taxi's window like schools of oceanic fish in a seaquarium. It was a beautiful dream, drenched in surrealism. I knew it was real, but I tried to understand why these unbelievable coincidences kept happening.

The band was packing up by the time I arrived at the Copacabana. Renee was putting away the last of her brochures. The event had ended, and the straggling drunks who hadn't connected with any new dates stumbled out.

Carlos had just finished wrapping up his electrical cords as I approached, and was putting his guitar into its case. I must have looked as if I was either drunk or had just seen a ghost.

"Carlos, it's hard to believe what just happened," I said.

"Are you okay?"

"Yeah, I'm okay. Do you remember the story I told you before I left earlier—about Renee and the *Layla* album cover?"

"Yes."

"When I got to Scott's party at Harry's apartment, this painting was on the wall right above where Scott was playing guitar," I said, taking out my phone to show Carlos the picture.

Carlos wiped the chills off his arms and said, "Damn, bro, that is freaky! What's up with that?"

"I don't know. It's just too weird," I said. "I have to go talk with Renee."

"Don't tell her about the painting."

"I won't. Definitely not," I said, starting to walk over to her.

"How was your night?" I asked.

"Fine. Yours?"

"Fine."

I gave her a hand packing up the rest of her booth and asked, "Did you drive in or take the ferry?"

"I drove."

"If I gave you $20 for gas, would you give me a ride?"

"You don't have to give me $20, silly. It would be great if you could help me get all this stuff to my car, though. My shoulder hasn't completely healed from the operation yet, and I'm parked four long blocks away."

I slung the heavy road case with the display in it over my shoulder.

We left the club, heavy rain pouring down on the dark streets of Manhattan. Within minutes we were totally drenched, hair dripping wet, our feet mopping up the puddles on the West Side.

Renee shouted over the raucous rain. "I don't know what I would have done without you tonight! You're like an angel appearing out of nowhere to help me!"

She was worn out from a full evening of having to speak with drunken, hopeful customers at the bar. Her labored breathing took all her remaining strength, from carrying the heavy packages of brochures.

"Do you know we have a mutual friend?" I asked.

"*Really?* Who?"

"Marina Ashley."

"Oh, Marina. How is she? We used to see each other at modeling jobs all the time. She's so nice!"

"Yes, she is a very nice person."

"How do you know her?"

"I lived outside Philly last year, and we had mutual friends."

"I haven't seen her in at least a year. Didn't she move out of New York?"

"Yes, she did."

"You have to send her a big hello when you talk to her next."

"I really don't talk with her that much since I moved back to New Jersey."

We trudged along. The rain had subsided somewhat.

"Are we close?" I asked, panting and switching the road case to my other shoulder.

"About halfway there, I think." She stopped at a street corner to get her bearings on the location of her car. "I think it's two more blocks this way."

I'd been mentally hashing out how to bring up the past. "I really don't know what happened to us."

"What do you mean?"

"Well, when we first met it seemed like there was a nice vibe between us. And then something changed."

Renee answered, "I had my operation."

"I know. But . . . ." I could sense that nothing was registering with her.

We finally arrived at her car, parked on a dark side street, and unloaded the waterlogged show materials into her trunk.

She said, "I don't know what I would have done without you. You really are like an angel in my life today."

"Well, I'd like to be more than just an angel in your life."

She looked me straight in the eye, "I'm not ready for a relationship."

I was obviously disappointed.

"I'm sorry," she said.

The next day, Scott called. "So glad you could make it to Harry's party. What was up with the painting?"

I poured out the whole sad story. "It just doesn't make sense to me. Why would all of those magical things happen for me to connect with Renee again just for her to tell me that she's not ready for a relationship?"

"I don't know," Scott responded. Neither did I . . . .

Chapter 36

Harrison House

A few days later, I had a New Age trade show to do outside Philadelphia. I texted Marina that I'd be in the area. She suggested that we meet at the Boro Bean, the coffee shop where we used to meet in Hopewell. I entered Hopewell into my new GPS and started driving. The GPS directed me to take a route I'd never taken before, but I trusted it. It's always right.

The drive from Cliffside Park to Hopewell, New Jersey is usually ninety minutes. After two hours of driving, I began wondering if something wasn't right, but the GPS finally pronounced I should get off the New Jersey Turnpike. None of it looked familiar. The first traffic light I came to turned red. As I waited for it to change, I glanced across the street. The Harrison House Diner sat before me.

"I don't remember that on my way to Hopewell," I said aloud to myself.

It seemed comical to me that it was called the Harrison House Diner—and there I was, on my way to see Marina.

After driving a little further, I realized I was almost out of gas and stopped at a gas station next to a sign saying Hopewell, two miles. Another car pulled in next to me. A middle-aged woman stepped out of her car to start filling her tank.

"Excuse me," I said, "can you tell me when I get to Main Street in Hopewell, do I turn right or left to get to the Boro Bean?"

"The what?" asked the woman.

"The Boro Bean. It's a coffee shop right in downtown."

"There is no Boro Bean in Hopewell."

"Ma'am, I've been there before."

I could tell she was running out of patience and didn't want to be bothered. "Look, young man, I've lived here all my life, and I can guarantee you there is no Boro Bean coffee shop in downtown Hopewell or any part of Hopewell."

I texted Marina. "Hey there. My GPS took me a different way and I think I'm in Hopewell, but there seems to be no Boro Bean here. What's the address?"

Marina was driving and couldn't answer the text, so while I was waiting, I entered the Boro Bean Cafe in Hopewell, New Jersey into my GPS, and it told me that I was 3.5 hours away. How could that be possible? The GPS clarified that there were *two* Hopewells in New Jersey, and the one I was in was close to the Delaware Memorial Bridge and the Atlantic Ocean. The town right next to it is Harrison, New Jersey! I was trying to have lunch with Marina in Hopewell but was taken to Harrison, New Jersey!

I texted her what had happened and that I wouldn't be able to get there in time, since she had to pick up Zarina from school about an hour from then.

She texted back, "What a bummer! I made you a pot of soup!"

It just wasn't meant to be.

Chapter 37

Something in the Way She Moves

A few weeks later, I was at the spa show in Dallas and met a Chilean woman named Candace. She wasn't blonde or blue-eyed, but she was strikingly beautiful and an incredible dancer. There was one thing getting in the way, though . . . she only spoke about twenty words of English and I only remembered about fifty words of Spanish. Sometimes it would take me five minutes just to say one sentence to her because I'd have to keep looking up words in my English/Spanish dictionary.

To release the frustration she would sometimes say, "Mi amor, cantar para mi." This meant, "Honey, sing for me." Every time she'd ask me, this one song always came to my mind, "Something," which I always called Something in the Way She Moves. I would sing it for her three different times.

Yet each time I could never remember the words of the second verse so I just mumbled something. Then at the chorus I would be back on track with, *"You're asking me will my love grow . . ."* and I'd sing it all the way to the end.

After the fourth time I sang it for her over the phone, I decided to look the song up on YouTube to find out what the words were in the second verse. I got such a strong inner direction to do this that I just followed it. There were so many versions of the song, but I clicked on the first one. This was the version George played with Eric Clapton and Leon Russell, one of the last songs at The Concert for Bangladesh. During the second verse, George messed up the words. They were in the exact place where I could never remember the words!

A few days later, while I was listening to the radio, I heard an interview with Paul McCartney. Someone called in to the station and asked him, "Do you still get nervous about making a mistake while performing?" Paul replied that he was a perfectionist, but that sometimes, when you do make a mistake, it makes that version special because that is how people remember it.

Chapter 38

Just Be

The week after the Eckankar seminar in April 2013, I was recording "I Am Loved" at Brian Bart's studio on Lake Minnetonka, outside of Minneapolis.

One morning, Brian slept late and forgot to leave the door unlocked. Since I had nothing to do, I drove down the street to the Brighton Bay Cafe in Navarre, a tiny town next to the lake. It was 8:00 a.m. and there were eight retirees, men and women, sitting around a long table. Since there was nowhere else to sit, I sat down in the empty seat on the end next to them. They invited me into their conversation and made me part of the gang. Life was good.

After about ten minutes, a feeling of contentment came over me. I stopped thinking. I wasn't sure what had brought on this beautiful feeling. I'd just experienced an amazing performance in front of 3,000 people a few days earlier, and had the chance to spend time with many of my friends at the seminar.

I also got to see my stepdaughter, Wendy, again. She was a popular waitress at an Italian restaurant in Minnesota. We joked around, shared our troubles and dreams, and had a great time catching up and reconnecting.

A new creative outlet had opened up for me with the *Musical Affirmations* CDs. These were positive mantras that I created with melodies and set them to relaxing music. I actually created these for myself to help me heal during the increasing difficulties of my life.

My Mind Is Clear, My Mind Is Calm was the first CD. This was my mantra that I wrote on Post-It notes all over my apartment to help me deal with the stress and changes in my life. It was the opposite of how I really felt and I wanted to try to change that. I figured that if I listened to a CD of me singing it to myself while I painted or was driving in my car, the words would go deeper into my conscious and subconscious mind. It was one continuous song for an hour. This way I could also sell it to the massage therapists who needed their CDs to be an hour long.

The music was very calming and put the listener in a sort of peaceful trance as I sang these words in a soft, gentle, almost monk-like tone that were mixed into the background of the music every three or four minutes. Eventually, after listening to it over and over, I started to convince myself that my mind was clear and calm. The more I sang along with it inside myself, the more these positive words became a part of my being and my body relaxed because it kept hearing from my brain that everything was clear and calm. I said it washed out my brain because that sounded much better than calling it "brainwashing myself."

The second affirmation CD was called *I Have Everything I Need and All Is Well*. I made this after the reality of the foreclosure of my mansion in Minneapolis finalized. I lost my $100,000 down payment and for seven years paid a $4,000-a-month mortgage for nothing. Now I was sharing a two-bedroom apartment near Ft. Lee, New Jersey with a roommate, so I could drive to shows on the East Coast and keep my expenses down and save money on flights. At least I had my own bathroom.

I found that the more I listened to this CD, the more I became at peace with my situation. I did have everything I needed as long as I stayed focused on the present moment and didn't stress out about my future.

▲ ▲ ▲

One of my friends invited me over to her house to watch the second DVD of George's HBO special, Martin Scorsese's *Living in the Material World*, and I accepted the chance to see it again. It had been a year since the first cable broadcast, and I got the nudge that this would be a good thing for me to watch again. Since my life had been in such turmoil the previous year it almost felt like I was watching it for the first time—as I didn't remember most of it. I was really surprised to see George speaking about the benefits of mantras, how they help to re-program our brain and how he repeated one mantra over and over at one point for three days! I had written and recorded my "My Mind Is Clear, My Mind Is Calm" a year before that HBO special was aired! And I found out later that George Harrison's last solo album was called *Brainwashed*!

Mantras were a useful aspect of Hinduism, which was George's spiritual path and a big part of his life. Some of these were thousands of years old and were written to help people learn how to live a better life—positive, guiding affirmations telling people the way to live life to its fullest. Since these words were actually sung, once the melody was remembered in the brain, people never forgot the words. So over many generations, mothers sang these to their children, who grew up to be adults, who sang them to *their* children. On holidays these were also sung in temple celebrations, and this is why these mantras are still around thousands of years later.

Was George helping me to create the Musical Affirmations, these new mantras in English for the spiritual benefit of people now as well as in the future just as the Hindus and many other religions had done? It certainly seemed so.

These first two CDs became my best-selling CDs because there was nothing like it in English on the planet. I actually sold out of both of them at four shows in a row at one point. That never happened with my other CDs. The musical medicine I had created for myself was now started to help people all over the world. These affirmations were forging something positive into my life, mentally and financially and little by little I started to feel better.

▲ ▲ ▲

I also started to realize that some of the lyrics that I had written in the songs for Marina the previous year were now playing out in my life. These next words are in "I'm Still Missing You":

I wish I really knew why so many people cry.
Oh, I wish I could sing the world a lullaby.

As I was describing the Musical Affirmations to customers at my shows, I had been saying, "These CDs are like adult lullabies to help people deal with stress, anxiety, and changes in life that feel like they are out of our control."

I'd also explain that we can only hear one song in our brain at a time, so when they listened to these CDs, their negative thoughts were blocked out because they were subconsciously singing along with the positive affirmations. We can't hold both a negative thought and a positive thought at the same time. Maybe this was also why I started to feel more positive about my life again.

I met a doctor/scientist in New York City at one of the Braco healing events I was performing at and she explained the science behind this. In simple terms, "Words are stored in the right side of the brain while music is stored and appreciated in the left side of the brain. A musical affirmation triggers the left and right side of the brain at the same time and it becomes more than twice as powerful.

"A perfect example is elderly people with Alzheimer's disease who can't remember their own names, or their spouses or children's names, but can still sing all the words to 'Amazing Grace' from beginning to end! This is because when words are attached to a melody the brain never forgets them."

This ancient wisdom was resurfacing to help heal people using modern mechanisms like CDs and downloads as the delivery system.

I started exhibiting at the psychological conventions and was the only one with any kind of musical affirmation. I was a hit! The first thing every psychologist did with a new patient was give them an affirmation, to convince themselves the opposite of their negative situation was possible through a positive mantra. How many psychologists were there in the world? These could easily be sung in any language. This gave me hope that I could survive the economic crisis and the digital age. Maybe life was leading me to an island that the dragon hadn't found yet.

▲ ▲ ▲

I finished another tour with Braco, the healer from Croatia. I could feel the effects of the positive energy from the presentations and the people attending appreciated what I had to offer. So I gave myself permission to stop worrying—to stop thinking about everything we feel the need to always think about—and just *be*. It was unique to not think for a while. It was wonderful, peaceful, exhilarating, and just nice!

One by one the breakfast crew left the café where I was having coffee, leaving me there by myself in bliss. I wrote down the words to "Just Be" on a napkin to describe where I was at.

It's been a long time
Such a long time

Since I had nothing on my mind
So I could just be
Just be

I took the long way
Down this highway
And I realized today
It's all about peace
Just peace

At least an hour and a half went by with me gently singing these words inside myself. I was in the zone. I decided to go across the street to a little café with a few tables outside and sit down. After sitting for a few minutes, and since no one had shown up to open the place yet, I retrieved my guitar from the car and started putting the words together with a chord pattern that seemed to follow the words nicely. I recorded it on my iPhone so I wouldn't forget it. Although it was an unusually cold April, I sat there at that metal table on the main street in Navarre in my heavy winter jacket.

Eventually, Brian called me and I resumed work on *I Am Loved.* A few weeks later I recorded *With Every Breath I Take, My Body Heals Itself,* and then *It's Time to Let Go/I'm OK.* I was pleased; three CDs in two months, in addition to traveling to shows and performances on the weekend.

The sound of my guitar on these recordings had morphed into something new that I had never heard before. Sometimes I would listen back to some of what I had played and not recall playing any of it. It didn't even sound like me. It sounded like George, or how George would have played through my hands—the tones, the choice of notes, the melodies, and the choice of notes to bend. My music had definitely taken a step up. I now had a new producer guiding me, a mystical invisible partner who knew much more than I thought I knew about creating great music. And this new music moved people.

▲▲▲

A few months and many cities later, I decided to take the July 4th weekend off and visit Washington, D.C. There were so many interesting places to see, and the weather was excellent. One morning I was at my friend Terrie's place, playing her daughter Sammy's guitar. I found myself playing "Just Be" over and over. The tone of her guitar was very pure and surprisingly reminded me of George Harrison's sound. Sammy commented that the peace in that song was so moving that it made her cry.

That same afternoon, we were sitting by the pool and I saw a cloud form in the sky. It looked exactly like the head and body of a male lion with a long mane. There was a swirling infinity symbol in its head, very similar to some of my paintings. The wind blew it across the sky above me in slow motion, so it looked like the lion's outstretched body was running. It lasted so long I pointed it out to Terrie, who could see it as well.

The following morning, as I was playing the song again, I had the thought that since our day was full of sightseeing, and there were no plans yet for the evening, maybe we could see if there were any recording studios in the area I could use to record the song. Google gave us the number for Lion and

Fox Recording, and it was very close. I debated whether to get all involved with recording on my only weekend off, but what were the odds that there would be a studio with the word "lion" in it the day after I saw a cloud lion in the sky?

I called the studio and spoke with Jim Fox. He said that considering it was a holiday weekend and normal people don't work on holiday weekends, the studio was available. It was a professional facility and Jim was an excellent engineer who had been in the business for forty years. In passing, he said that the area was famous because years ago, the Beatles played their first concert in America right down the street. Go figure.

A few hours later, in the middle of the session, a phone call came in for Jim. I was surprised he took the call. He was on it for at least fifteen minutes. It's not normal protocol for an engineer to do this when a client is there paying for the time. As I began to wonder how much longer he was going to interrupt our session, he wound down his conversation and said, "Okay, Harrison, I need to get back to work here," and hung up.

I asked, "You were on the phone with a guy named Harrison?"

"Yes, that was one of my clients from San Francisco. His first name is Harrison."

Terrie and I just looked at each other and smiled.

A few hours later, I decided it would be good to hire a keyboard player. Jim recommended an African musician named George who quickly came over and did a great job.

The two names of the people who interjected their energy into that recording were George and Harrison.

"Just Be" was finished on July 6, 2013.

Chapter 39

Tom Petty and the Number 42

I had the number 42 in my head for days. I flew to Los Angeles for shows and meetings, and slept during the first half of the flight. I woke up with three things in mind: my headache; the George Harrison special which had aired again on HBO recently; and the thought that, since I was going to be in Los Angeles and Tom Petty lived there, I needed to find someone who knew him. Tom Petty was one of the on-screen narrators in Scorsese's film because he was a close friend of George's. They even started a band, together with fellow music greats Jeff Lynne, Roy Orbison, and the legendary Bob Dylan, called the Traveling Wilburys.

I landed, picked up my rental car, and headed up to the valley. I had been there a few weeks earlier and reconnected with an old friend, Dave Green. Dave is a sharp-looking, thin black man who rides a Harley and plays drums. I had known him for twenty years, on and off, from the meditation group I belonged to in L.A. We'd never gotten together for lunch, but decided to remedy that.

The weather was perfect, a gorgeous Southern California day. As I drove on the 405 North and came up over the Hollywood hills, it came to me again, *I need to find someone who is connected to Tom Petty.*

Dave and I met at Crave on Ventura Boulevard, just east of Laurel Canyon. He's one of those guys who never seems to get older.

After we greeted each other, I said, "Dave, I never really knew what you did for a living. What do you do?"

His response gave me another shiver. "Oh, I've been working as a drum technician for the past twelve years . . . for Tom Petty."

The following day, I jumped into my car and turned on the radio. At that exact moment, the announcer spoke as I pulled out of the parking lot. "You know that John Lennon and Paul McCartney were not the only great songwriters in the Beatles. Our next song in our Top 100 countdown is by George Harrison, and it's number 42. Don't go anywhere. We'll be right back after this commercial break with 'Something.'"

▲▲▲

As time and events carried me to the end of the summer of 2013, I began to feel haunted by the fear that all my experiences with George Harrison would not be believed. Some of my very good friends, who are a little older than I am, were such deep, die-hard George Harrison fans that they couldn't handle hearing about all this. George had been their hero in every sense of the word. The evidence in my stories was undeniable, but what was my motivation in sharing them with the world? If they were so sacred and real, why did I want to make a book out of it for the public? They thought I should just keep the story to myself.

It all culminated in the middle of another sleepless August night. I was reflecting on what I've learned over the years through my opportunities and hard knocks. From the time of the early days of my career in an AC/DC tribute band, there was craziness. It was expected. I'd dress up like Angus Young in his signature blue suit and shorts and run all over the stage non-stop while we played a ninety-minute show each night. I was a hyperactive kid, anyway, so this was a perfect fit.

I stuck at that until I grew bored, sick, and tired of that gig and chucked it all to follow in Yanni's footsteps, playing the Venice Beach scene. After I played on the beach all day and didn't even raise enough money to cover the cost of the parking meter, I met Lisa, a harpist, and we did better playing together. It was there I got the crazy idea to try playing two recorders at once. The magic ensued. Crowds gathered. We pulled together makeshift cassette tapes that sold and sold, and everything I touched turned to gold for years. Over one million CDs and downloads were sold, and over ten thousand therapists of all kinds and hospitals used my music every day to heal their patients.

Then came the disappointing relationships and the fate of falling in love with Marina, just six months after my breakup with Emma. The Internet, Napster, and the collapse of the music industry as we knew it all took a toll. Following were the less-than-successful new venues I tried, and eventually the loss of my treasured house and family. All I'd built over almost two decades slowly eroded. Then came a lawsuit from my ex-manager—who had first been my friend—trying to work over the legal system by suing me for $125,000.

How many disappointments can a human being take? I was working harder than I ever had, and struggling in an uphill battle in every area of my life. The dragon of my own fears, which was wondering what would become of my life, came closer and closer at every turn now. It loomed larger than ever, with the court dates approaching. Its visage wore the changing faces of doubters and betrayers, friends and family—some who really thought I was crazy, and some who thought I was experiencing something so incredible and supernatural that they would have given anything for just one moment of it.

For some reason, I believe that George Harrison chose me as a mortal entity with which to make new music. I believe he also chose me to date dear Marina, and help her regain her self-confidence so she could move forward in her life. He continually popped up in my life at the most bizarre, perfect moments—times when I needed to laugh, times when I was close to the edge, and times that led to the countless adventures and miracles his presence has created in my life.

I'm thinking these happenings can't just be for me. They must be for me to share with all of the people who wish he was still here—smiling, making amazing music, and doing things that made this world we live in a more spiritually evolved place. There wasn't much yoga and meditation in the Western world before he exposed us to it. Now there are yoga studios in almost every city.

The idea of self-realization was relatively unknown to American mainstream culture before he helped bring it to our attention. He used his celebrity to bring attention to what he felt were more important things that could make the world better. I'm sure if he had remained a Catholic, he would have been declared a saint just for what he did to help all of the starving people of Bangladesh. That concert and video raised over ten million dollars at the time of their benefit. Nowadays, that would be more like one hundred million dollars.

In my opinion, some of the most incredible Beatles songs from the band's late-1960s releases were written by George. I thought their most romantic love song was "Something." Their most spiritual song to me was "Within You Without You." Their most uplifting song was "Here Comes the Sun." Their most epic guitar hero song was "While My Guitar Gently Weeps." His quiet strength and support of John and Paul, when stacked alongside the rock-steady beat and affectionate loyalty of drummer Ringo Starr, truly held and defined the body and mind and spirit of the Beatles. How could anyone ever fail, having such a selfless and generous soul by their side?

Sometimes I wondered if I'd ever see George again. And yet I was often afraid that I *would* see George again—*as a ghost*! But as time went on, I really wanted to get over that fear.

▲ ▲ ▲

My own experiences with the black shadow of my own life's dragon started to drive out every good thought in my mind. Every good memory fell under the crushing weight of so many fears and disappointments. I felt helpless in the struggle. Unarmed and defenseless. The beast bit me hard. The blackness coursed through me, surrounded me, carried me in a torrential hurricane of doubt, and it took every ounce of my remaining strength to cry out, "Help me!" and I finally fell asleep, exhausted.

Sleep brought me no relief, though. In my dream, I was still trying frantically to work everything out. In desperation, I pleaded for help inwardly.

Then I began to feel a shift . . . a gentle presence. A calming peace began to take over. And I saw George's face once again. And then he was standing right in front of me.

"I need your help."

George replied with grace, comforting me. "I've been helping you. I am helping you. And I will continue helping you."

Then I woke up. The overwhelming sense of love, relief, and support brought me to tears. I cried for ten minutes.

Chapter 40

Victoria and the Agent

I was in the middle of a two-month tour of so many cities that I had to tear a page out of an airplane magazine to keep track. Michigan for two weeks, then Los Angeles, Michigan again, Las Vegas, San Diego, Houston, then back to Michigan.

I had planned on visiting my brother Howie in Ohio, but he decided last-minute to go on a golfing trip with his buddies. I arrived at Detroit Airport at ten o'clock on Monday morning. My next show was way up north in Borne, Michigan on Friday. I now had four days with nothing to do, and I didn't have any friends anywhere close.

The shuttle bus took me to my car in the long-term parking lot. The driver dropped me off and quickly drove away, leaving me standing there among a thousand cars, wondering where I should go and what I should do.

Bewildered, I looked up at the sky to talk to God and ask for direction, which was comical. Why do we always look up at the sky to communicate with the Creator? If Divine Energy is everywhere, wouldn't it be just as good to look under my car? Anyway, I stood there for fifteen minutes and nothing happened.

I decided to open up the car door and sit down. "Okay, you've got me. I am in your hands. I surrender. Please guide me to what I am supposed to do and where I am supposed to go."

Nothing.

Hmmm. After ten minutes of sitting there without getting any direction, I decided that since I had to figure something out and it may take a while, it might be better for me to go to the hotel right next to the long-term parking and use their computer in the lobby. That would be better than sitting in my car and the screen would be easier to see than my iPhone.

I pulled in, parked, and walked into the lobby like I owned the place, so they wouldn't question what I was doing there. I sat down at the computer in the business center.

"I'm still open for directions," I said, speaking to the universe.

Nothing.

Of all the states, I had spent the least amount of time in Michigan—and then only in Detroit and Ann Arbor. The idea of spending four days in a hotel by myself because I didn't know anyone around there sounded awful. I did a Google search to pull up a state map, and I combed it for a clue to something with which I might have a connection.

I see Ann Arbor, Novi, Grand Rapids . . . *hmmm* . . . Traverse City. It's way up north and looked like it was about an hour from Borne. So why does Traverse City sound familiar?

About nine years before, when I was in the middle of making the film *Village of Dreams* in Rothenburg, Germany, I was flying back and forth for seven months. It was putting a strain on my relationship with Emma, so to try to make some personal time possible for us, I decided to fly her to London and meet her there so we could have three much-needed days together.

On the first night, we decided to go to the theatre district to see if any tickets were available for that night. It was close to 8:00 p.m., when the shows were starting and, fortunately, there were two tickets left in the whole city. They were for *Mamma Mia!* I was not a big fan of ABBA, but Emma was excited so I bought them and we ran as fast as we could so we wouldn't miss the beginning.

When we arrived at the theatre a few blocks away, the show was about to start and we sat down in the last two seats in the top row. These must have been the worst seats in the theatre, which was why they were the only two tickets left in the whole city! Sitting next to us in the nosebleed seats was a woman about our age and an older man. We introduced ourselves to Victoria and Ben, her business partner—two people in town for a book convention. Then the show started.

It was amazing! We loved it.

During intermission, we continued our conversation with our neighbors. When I told her why I was in Europe, she said, "Why don't you pop over to Bologna next month? I can get you a pass to get in. Have you ever been to a book fair?" I said I hadn't.

Then the second half of the show started. We all thoroughly enjoyed it. Afterwards, she gave me her business card and said she lived in Traverse City, Michigan, and if I was ever in the area I should give her a call.

I had never heard of Traverse City, but honest to God, over the past nine years whenever I would hear the word Michigan, I would think of it. I'm not kidding.

So there I was in the hotel next to the long-term parking lot at Detroit Airport looking at a state map on the computer in the lobby. *Am I really going to call this woman?*

I looked in my iPhone, but didn't have her number. *Damn.*

But by chance, I did have an email address, so I sent a text message to her, not knowing if that would work.

"Hi Victoria. It's David Young. Remember me? We met in London at *Mamma Mia!* nine years ago. I just landed at Detroit Airport and I don't have to be in Borne for my next show until Friday. What are you guys up to? Wanna get together?"

I hit "Send" with low expectations, since I hadn't ever sent a message like that.

Two minutes later, her reply arrived. "Hey, David! Great to hear from you. What are you doing? Wanna come to Traverse City and stay with us for a couple days? We have a spare bedroom."

This was music to my ears! "That sounds wonderful! My GPS says I'm about four hours away. I'll see you soon! Thanks so much," I replied.

"We are having family over for dinner and there's a ton of food, so don't eat."

"Okay, great." We sign off.

OHHHH MY GOD!

I drove up to their amazing place. Victoria and her husband, Matt, owned a literary review magazine called *Foreword Reviews*. They bought a very cool, old building with twelve-foot ceilings and renovated it, but left all of the old wood and put their offices for ten people on the top floor. Their living quarters were on the first floor, and it was huge. It actually used to be a cigar factory seventy-five years ago. It was so beautiful and artsy, like something out of *Architectural Digest*! One half of their giant living room was turned into an art gallery, with about fifteen paintings. They also used the space for events, with speakers and musicians for house concerts.

As I ate an incredible dinner, we spoke about how bizarre it was that we had met in London all those years ago. Then I was tired and went to sleep.

The next day, I told this whole story to Victoria.

They were very busy during the morning, working on their magazine, so I went walking around the town, which was on a giant lake. It was really beautiful and a tad touristy.

She invited me to have lunch with her, and we caught up with the past. She asked about Emma. I told her that we didn't make it, and that we had finally gotten over the numerous, terrible break-ups and wished each other well.

I mentioned that I had lived through an amazing story, and it was the perfect time for me to tell it to her since I was leaving that afternoon. It took almost two hours to tell her the whole story, and when I was done, she said it was one of the most incredible stories she'd ever heard. She told me she was going to connect me to an agent in California named Bill. Then we hugged goodbye and I drove off to the next city.

Fifteen minutes later, I received a message from Bill saying that anyone who had sold a million CDs was worth taking a meeting with and he left his phone number. I called him and told him fifteen minutes of my story. He said he was intrigued, and that his assistant would take down my information.

And fifteen minutes later, I had a representation contract from him via the iPhone. By the end of the day, we had a commitment from a publisher to put out the book. All of this happened within twenty-four hours of George telling me in a dream that he was helping me.

The following week, I flew to L.A. and met with Bill. While I was there, he contacted a film agent in Hollywood who knew the Beatles! This is the letter Bill sent to him:

"David is a new Waterside client whose background and story will interest you. He is based on the East Coast and only in L.A. this week. David has sold in excess of one million New Age music albums, and is known as the two-flute musician. David has an incredible story to tell that includes his experiences over the last three years in channeling both the spirit and musical talent of famous Beatle, George Harrison.

"The first draft of the book is nearly complete, but the film or stage musical will be a much bigger event. I would like you to meet with him, and if possible, hear his whole story. David is a gifted storyteller, and kept Gayle and me enthralled for about two hours, so best you meet him around 5 p.m., so you can hear the whole story. My intuition is that we take the manuscript, create coverage, and pitch immediately for film since, as we know, the actual book would not come out for at least a year. Just email David directly or call him to set up a time to meet."

Then I got the call from the film agent's office, had the appointment, and the manuscript for the book you're now reading was soon in his hands.

Later that day, I was driving in my car, taking in all of this. I had never had a literary representative before, and I was excited. After telling all of these incredible coincidences, or George-incidences as I called them to my close friends, everyone says that there will never be an end to it. The thought of the book coming out, and the possibility of it being made into a film, so the people of the world would know that George is still alive and well would be a way for those who love and appreciate him to connect with him in another way. In order for all of this to have happened, there must be life after death.

Since I have made numerous music videos and two short films, I was aware that making a film requires a big budget. As I was driving I thought to myself, *This is gonna take time, money, and a whole lot of it.*

I got a strong nudge to turn on the radio, and there was George was singing loud and clear from the song, "I've Got My Mind Set on You," written by Rudy Clark: *"It's gonna take money-ey. A whole lot of spending money."*

I laughed and sang along, then said out loud, speaking to my radio, "There's never a dull moment, is there?"

Chapter 41

Grandma Returns

I flew back to New York and called my friend Pam Lubell. Pam used to be in the movie business, and before she had her kids, worked for Miramax Films. She was close friends with Scott and Harry, and lived on the Upper West Side. Over the past two years, I had told her everything that had happened.

Pam also had two daughters who both sang and I had really connected with Sage, her older daughter who was sixteen and very mature for her age. We had written three songs together the previous year. I had intended to produce these songs for her but my life took off on this giant adventure of traveling "all over everywhere," as I described it.

I met Pam for dinner, and afterwards we took a walk. I hadn't seen in her six months so there was a lot to catch up on.

She said, "You missed another great jam with Scott and all the guys from the meadow last week. We had a big party for John Lennon's birthday."

The meadow referred to the meadow in Central Park, where I had met Scott when I first moved back to the New York area about two years before.

"I didn't know it was John Lennon's birthday. When was that?" I asked.

"October 9th."

There's that number 9 again, I thought.

Then I realized that my publisher Bob and I had finished the first draft of the book on October 9th. I thought it was significant that we emailed the final manuscript to Bill on October 9th, because then Barry would receive it on 10/10/10, which was three years to the day from when I first met Marina playing football.

"Oh, my God, we finished *Channeling Harrison* and sent it off to the agent on John Lennon's birthday."

"So . . . ?"

"Let me ask you something, Pam. How much do you truly believe of my story? Fifty percent, eighty percent, or one hundred percent?"

She said, "One hundred percent."

"Thanks. After everything that has happened this past month, I finally completely believe it too!" I said.

"It's the most incredible story I've ever heard," Pam added.

My cell phone rang. "Pam, excuse me. My publisher is on the phone."

Bob tried to contain his excitement. "Barry just told me he wants to take this to Peter Asher, and may ask him to be the executive producer of the film! This is big!"

I knew that Barry was business partners with Peter Asher in the 1970s. Back in 1968, Peter had been appointed as the Artists & Repertoire (A&R) department head for the Beatles' quickly-formed independent label, Apple Records. The first artist that Peter signed to Apple was none other than prolific American singer/songwriter James Taylor, and he then went on to produce other great soft-rock singer/songwriters of the 1970s such as Linda Ronstadt, Bonnie Raitt, Neil Diamond, and a great many others. He was the only music business manager that *Time* magazine put on the front cover because his influence of bringing new music to the world in the '70s was so profound.

Bob asked, "How do you know all this about Peter Asher?"

"Peter has an incredible show called *A Musical Memoir of the '60s and Beyond.* In it, he tells stories about how he found James Taylor, and even how John Lennon met Yoko Ono in London at the Indica bookshop and arts gallery that Peter co-owned along with artist John Dunbar and writer Barry Miles. It's amazing! He sings, too. Do you remember the song, "A World Without Love"?

"Yes," Bob answered.

"Peter was the singer of that song. He had a duo called 'Peter and Gordon.' When they got their record deal in the '60s after they were found playing in a college pub, they needed one more song for their album. Peter was sharing an attic apartment with Paul McCartney because Paul was dating his sister, Jane Asher. Paul wanted to get away from all the craziness at the Beatles' house on Green Street in Mayfair, where everyone lived for a brief time and practiced together. So Jane's parents let him live in the other apartment in the attic, in the room next to Peter. They became close friends. Paul used to sing songs around the house and Peter was very fond of one of them in particular. It was, 'A World Without Love.' Since Peter and Gordon needed one final song to finish their album, Peter asked Paul if they could record that one. It became the number one song in the world."

"How can you possibly know all this, David?"

"Because one of my closest friends, Jeff, who is more of a brother than a friend, is Peter's piano player in the show. I've seen it twice and loved it! But Jeff is such a die-hard Beatles fan and George is his hero. He can't stand to even hear me talk about this!"

Bob said, "This is incredible. We really have to get a synopsis to Barry by Monday to give to Peter Asher. I started something, and I just emailed it to you."

"Okay. I'm with my friend Pam and she was in the movie business. I'll ask her to help me with it. I have an art show to do tomorrow that I need to get up for at six a.m., so I can get there early to set up."

Pam then asked me, "What in the world was *that* about?"

"We have to go back to your apartment and write up a synopsis for *Channeling Harrison*."

We walked a few blocks.

Pam and I arrived at her apartment, and we wrote the synopsis with Bob on speaker-phone.

Then Bob said, "I have a good friend who is a trusted psychic named Cathy, and I asked her to see if she could make contact with George. She came over, and went out onto the deck for a half-hour to meditate and connect with him. Soon after, George came into her inner vision and she asked, 'David wants to know what this is all about.'"

"George answered her, 'There are too many layers to explain it. And if I tell you too much it could get in the way of David's unfoldment. This needs to happen naturally. David is doing what he is supposed to be doing, and this will be a long and ongoing experience.'"

Pam and I finished up the synopsis, and I took a cab back to my apartment in New Jersey.

▲ ▲ ▲

The following morning, I went over to my mom's to pick up some boxes of CDs that had been shipped to her. I woke her up.

Mom said, "Something happened Thursday night before you got home. I was lying in my bed dozing off, and I felt Grandma's presence in the room as if she wanted to tell me something. She said that she had encouraged you to just have faith. Everything was going to be alright. She said, 'I came to David when he needed me.'"

Over the years my mom had told me many times that Grandma was still with her in spirit, and I can honestly say that I never took her seriously.

I started to cry because I never told my mom that two years before, in the depth of my depression, I had a dream where I saw Grandma. It was after I made the painting that later turned out to be the design of George's jacket.

Chapter 42

Goodness

I flew to Hawaii to recoup for a week and visit Sophia, a friend from the music business in Los Angeles, who I reconnected with and was there on vacation. Like everything else in this experience, though, something was bringing me there for a reason, and I wasn't aware what that reason was or what would happen next. But after all of this, I was getting closer and closer to truly believing my experiences, though my logical mind did everything possible to dismiss them a day or so later.

I have to say that I've grown accustomed to the miracles that were occurring and continue to take place in my life. When they happened, although they surprised me, I was ready, for them. I saw the divine comedy in the fact that George, somehow, had the power to set these things up at the perfect time. I really couldn't understand how it was all possible. Sometimes these magical moments occurred so that I could see something that connected pieces in the puzzle. Other times they were there so that I could meet someone who would somehow play a part and have a place in all of this.

Eventually, the right people have been brought into my world to help me get this story out. As a result, people who were still spiritually connected to their past loved ones would not be afraid to start sharing their stories. I started to see a pattern in my life whenever I would share any of this with someone. After hearing one of my stories, people would always ask me, "What do you think George is trying to tell you?" I would always answer, "I'm not sure." Then they would say something like, "My brother died three years ago, but he's still connected to me. He's always around and I actually feel his presence in my heart. Sometimes he plants little clues for me here and there. I know with every ounce of my being that my brother still exists, even though he is no longer alive here in the material world."

Fifty years ago, if someone told too many people they were still connected to a grandmother who had passed away, or to a brother who died at a young age, they may even have been thought to be crazy. Some were institutionalized. Because of this, many people have remained afraid to share their special inner experiences with others. Maybe this book will help to erase that old thought pattern from world consciousness.

▲ ▲ ▲

Hawaii is a place like no other. I've been to so many places on this planet, and I've never been anywhere that exudes such goodness and positive energy.

I am told that George lived part of the time in Hawaii. George is remembered as being such a positive light in this world. I wondered if living in Hawaii re-energized his beautiful, compassionate soul with extra goodness, and that he then took this energy back out into the world and shared it through his music.

After a nice morning at the beach, watching the never-ending waves and soaking in the rays of the sun, my friend Sophia and I decided to get some lunch and drove a mile down the road to a coffee shop. It was 2:00 p.m., and the place was empty. The cordial owner, a kind man in his early sixties, got our order and we sat down in the other room filled with soft couches and beautiful island paintings all over the walls. There was an old piano up against the wall next to where we sat.

Earlier that day, I had been thinking about how many wonderful qualities Sophia had. I loved her long red hair. I had thought about telling her "I wouldn't change anything about you," as we lay on the beach blanket that I borrowed from the hotel.

As we waited for the food to be prepared, I sat down at the piano and tinkered. I really don't play the piano, and I struggle to find notes that sound right together. I had the idea to try to write a song about what I had thought of telling Sophia earlier. These are the words that came to me:

If I could change the world,
What I'd like to do
Is find a way
To make everyone smile like you

Make everyone laugh like you
Shine like you
There's so many things I would change in this world
But I wouldn't change anything about you

If I could change the world
I'd make it a brighter place
With sunshine and happiness on every face
And make us all one people sharing this place
I'd remove the race from the human race

There's so many things I would change in this world
But I wouldn't change anything about you

I recorded it onto Sophia's phone because there was no memory left on my phone.

I thought these words reminded me of something that John Lennon would have written. The second verse was almost like an extension of his 1971 song, "Imagine." Of all of the Beatles, I had for some reason always felt the least connection with John. Something about Ringo always made me smile whenever I saw him on TV. I don't know why.

I had met Paul and because of his amazing talent as a singer, songwriter, and performer, I had the highest respect for him. And I think one of the best live albums of all time was his 2002 release, *Back in the USA.*

George always made me think of spirituality and being focused, for some reason. And he just seemed like an example of pure goodness.

Our lunch arrived at the perfect time, just as I finished recording the song.

Afterwards, we drove back to another beach that Sophia wanted to show me and she parked the car.

Over the past month, I had started to tell my close friends who knew what was going on that I really wished I could communicate consciously with George. Psychic mediums did this kind of thing all of the time, and were given information that only family members or close friends would have known. It was no problem for him to appear to me, or give messages to me in my dreams that would magically manifest in my life a few days or weeks later. He seemed to be able to make the impossible possible, and I wanted to make whatever changes necessary inside myself so I could communicate more directly with him.

I got a strong inner direction to meditate, and told Sophia she could join me if she wanted to do so. Sophia was very spiritual, so she was completely comfortable with the idea.

I closed my eyes and sang HU, the ancient mantra that I had been using for thirty years. Soon enough, the peace I would always feel came to me and opened my heart. The gentle, loving spiritual vibrations I experience during these meditations is the same kind of energy that I put into my flute music. This is the real reason that I believe so many people love my CDs and never seem to tire of listening to them. It opens them up to this higher vibration.

I closed my eyes and began to go inward, feeling the peace that comes with meditation. Soon, I felt like there was this mountain of spiritual energy and strength in front of me. It was pure goodness.

I smiled and said aloud, "Goodness. He is pure goodness. He is like an angel of goodness."

I kept repeating the word "goodness" aloud, and then I received this knowingness in my mind and in my heart:

He is an angel of music. His love for music is beyond words. Music flows through him, like water from a waterfall. He received the enlightenment. He eventually got to the level of spiritual enlightenment like Krishna, like Buddha. Buddha means "the enlightened one."

In the same way as Krishna started as a man and then after his enlightenment he was able to appear to people and create miracles for them, this has been how George was able to create miracles in my life.

"Goodness," I repeated over and over.

"What am I supposed to do?" I asked him.

I felt this comforting energy that prompted me just to relax and enjoy the journey. *Just relax. All you have to do is just be.* I felt supported, as if by an immense mountain of spiritual strength.

After about fifteen minutes, I opened my eyes. As we sat in the car, coming back to the physical realm, I said, "I'm ready."

Sophia and I left the car in the parking lot and started to walk towards the beach. As we walked, I could see there was this deep blue horizon beyond the palm trees and the shade. It looked like an infinite sky stretching out forever, as far as my eyes could see.

I said, "I've made it. I don't need to worry anymore."

I took in the freshness of the ocean air with a long deep breath.

"There are no more dragons," I said out loud. "After everything I have struggled with and suffered with I have finally made it."

There were about a hundred feet to walk in order to get to the ledge that overlooked the ocean.

"Let's walk slowly," I said to Sophia. "I want to enjoy every moment of this journey to the fullest."

After we would take a few steps, I would stop just to breathe and take it all in. We reached the palm trees at the edge of the cliff, with the brilliant blue ocean water and sky in front of us. An island about a hundred yards off-shore protruded from the ocean. This huge rock was in the shape of a giant lizard's head. It looked sort of like a dragon. "The dragon is frozen. It's a solid mountain of rock now, and can't hurt me anymore."

I finally believed completely.

I wrote a song for George that summed up my whole experience. It's called "Perfection."

The perfect timing, the perfect place
Your miracles always put smiles on my face
I can't help but see them,
They're all over the place
Your miracles always put smiles on my face

It's perfection, sweet perfection
There's perfection in everything you do
It's perfection, pure perfection

There's perfection in everything you do

The perfect words, the perfect rhyme
I'm not sure how you do it every time
Everywhere I look it seems I find
Another miracle that seems to blow my mind

It's perfection, pure perfection
There's perfection in everything you do
There's perfection, sweet perfection
There's perfection in everything you do

All this goodness shows up every day
All this goodness is all a part of your grace
And each time I find myself on cloud nine
It's amazing, so amazing

Your perfection, sweet perfection
There's perfection in everything you do
It's perfection, pure perfection
There's perfection in everything you do

Epilogue

St. George and the Dragon

A friend of mine from New Jersey was flying to the city of Prague in the Czech Republic, and he asked if I would like to come along. How could I pass it up? Prague was a city I knew nothing about, and I had always heard it was one of the most beautiful cities in Europe. So I accepted.

This happened when my editor, Doug, was getting ready to send me the first draft of his updated version of the first eleven chapters of this book. When I opened the email, there were three paragraphs about St. George and the dragon. I closed the email, thinking I must have clicked on the wrong thing. There was no St. George or any dragon in my book. When I reopened it, though, St. George and the dragon were still there. I had no idea why Doug put that into the story. Since I have been living through this story I sent an email to Bob, my publisher.

"Bob, Doug just sent me the first eleven chapters of the book and he's gone through it. He added this whole thing about St. George and the dragon, and I don't know what to think of it. If you want to keep it in the story, keep it. I'm too close to it all by now and it's up to you. I am flying to Prague tomorrow for a week. Take care, David."

I should also tell you that on the day when the publishing deal manifested with Bob, I had to book a hotel through Priceline.com. I use "Name Your Own Price," which chooses the hotel after you give them your bid. On that day, the hotel that was randomly given to me was on Munson Boulevard in Michigan. Doug's last name is Munson. I have never heard of a street with that name. I took this as a sign from the universe that Doug was definitely supposed to be working with us on the book.

When I emailed my agent Bill that I was flying to Prague, he immediately emailed back that I should look up his friend Jim, who had moved there from California. This was only about a week after I had connected with Bill. Jim had no idea that I had written a book about my connection with George Harrison. He only knew that I played the flute, and made spiritual music for spas.

I arrived in Prague and Jim set up a lunch meeting at the Nostress Cafe, close to where he lived. Before I had a chance to tell Jim why I was there or how I knew Bill, I asked him, "Why did you move to Prague?"

Jim answered, "I was invited to a showing of an old film (not a premiere) of a movie shot in India by movie director Howard Worth. It was a film about Ravi Shankar, and it featured the Beatles—and especially George Harrison—throughout.

"It was shown in Ojai, California, where I was living at the time. I immediately became a friend of Howard's. The gentleman who invited me was Irving Walzer, who arranged for the film to be shown in early December 2001, in memory of George Harrison's death in November 2001.

"I had been traveling internationally and was tired and did not want to go. My wife, a film director, had passed away two years earlier. My secretary talked me into going, after she was called several times by Irv, who insisted that I needed to attend.

"Two weeks later, Howard introduced me to David Walker, another movie producer from Los Angeles, who expressed an interest to visit my home in Ojai, as it was a heritage property built in 1926 by the famous architect Wallace Neff.

"Howard brought David and his wife, Iveta, who was born in Slovakia, to visit my home on January 9, 2002. It so happened that her best friend, Inez, was visiting from Prague. Inez got out of the car, and I fell in love with her. I took her to dinner the next evening. She left the next morning for Prague.

"I took a plane a few days later to Prague and stayed there. I eventually sold my home in Ojai. We decided to work on renovating Chateau Mcely as business partners. We started in July 2003 and opened in May 2006. We were married on July 9, 2003 and our daughter Julia was born on June 30, 2006. So I attribute meeting my new wife and all the love and happiness I share with her to George Harrison, because I would have never gone to that film screening if he had not been in the film."

"Wow! What an incredible story! The number 9 is all over your story on the most important days, and that number has been involved ever since this whole thing started with him. Where is Chateau Mcely located?"

"It's about an hour outside Prague, high on a hill in the St. George forest."

Bill never knew this was how Jim met his wife. For the rest of the week, St. George and the dragon popped up at least five times a day, but that story is for another time.

▲▲▲

Just to illustrate that this story still continues, it is now October of 2013 as I write this. I am sitting at my publisher's computer, editing the final manuscript at the top of a hill in the Blue Ridge Mountains of Virginia. His house is on a dirt road with nine other houses, basically in the middle of nowhere.

After a long day of writing with George's energy driving the bus here, we had dinner and Bob's companion, Beth, gave me a copy of George Harrison's CD, *All Things Must Pass*. I had told her that I'd never heard that album. Then I left and got in my car to drive back to where I was staying.

A man with long white hair was walking on the left side of the road as I drove to the end of the road before I turned left. I got an inner urge to stop at the Stop sign and wait for him. When he walked up to my car, I was guided to ask him for directions—even though I had a GPS right next to me showing me how to get to where I needed to go.

After he gave me directions, since he had long hair like me, I asked him, "Are you a musician?"

He said, "No, I'm an engineer."

"Who have you worked with?"

"I was Eddie Offord's assistant engineer."

"Why does that name sound familiar?"

"Eddie was the sound engineer for Yes, and my friend Alan White was their drummer."

"Why does the name Alan White sound familiar?"

"Because Alan White played drums with George Harrison on his album, *All Things Must Pass*. He also played with John Lennon on his song, "Imagine.""

▲ ▲ ▲

People always ask me, "What do you think George is trying to tell you?" I really don't know why all of this has happened. I thought at certain points that I understood why, but as time passed and more things continued to unfold with him in my world, I have gotten to the place where I have accepted that this will just continue. My music is much better since he has been around. I can hear and feel the difference, especially in my songwriting. My songs seem to be more memorable now. And in my guitar playing he has inspired me to play melodies instead of just fast notes. In every way, he's given my talent direction. There is an inexhaustible amount of creativity that now flows through me.

Great and wonderful beings are always in this world and beyond, in and out of the physical—*angels*, if you will. I believe they will always be here. Not just for me, but for you, too. Why else would there be heroes of legend, spiritual guides and masters, and something in the way that music moves us?

In Memory of Mark Reale

Mark was the lead guitarist of Riot, a band that came from where I grew up in Brooklyn. Riot had the good fortune to put out four or five rock albums by different major record labels in the late '70s and early '80s. They were also the opening live concert act for many huge bands of the time like Rainbow, AC/DC, Black Sabbath, and Van Halen's sometime frontman, Sammy Hagar.

When I was in high school, I really didn't fit in anywhere. I loved music and played my recorder five or six hours a day to my Jethro Tull, Bad Company, Led Zeppelin, and Pink Floyd albums—but I hadn't learned how to play guitar yet.

My parents bought me a Carlo Robelli nylon string acoustic guitar along with four lessons from a teacher, whose name I'll leave out here. The first song he wanted me to learn was, "I Am Woman," sung by Helen Reddy. That was the exact opposite of what I wanted to play. I quit before the four lessons were over.

About a year later, one of my high school friends who played the drums told me that his older brother, Darryl Goldstein, was the roadie for a rock band called Riot. This was around the year 1975 and I was probably a junior in high school. Riot wasn't famous yet and they were practicing in Mark's basement in Flatbush, about three miles from where I lived. His older brother had invited us to a band rehearsal, and we tagged along in his car like excited puppies in the back seat of his car.

When we arrived and parked, you could already hear them practicing from all the way down the street. I had never heard anything that loud, or even remotely close to that cool.

Since we were just high school kids, they let us sit on the stairs on the way down to the basement. The room was filled with stacked Marshall amps and drums positioned along the back wall. The roadies got to lean against the wall and hang in the room as the band practiced. They let my friend and I sit on the stairs, out of sight. We weren't allowed in the main room.

The original four guys from the band—Mark Reale, the singer Guy Speranza, bassist Phil Fiet, and drummer Peter Bitelli all had long rock'n'roll hair and wore cool '70s-style musician-type clothes. After all, it *was* the '70s.

When Mark played his Les Paul electric guitar, he could make you cry from the heart and soul that he put into the way he bent the notes. But he could also make you feel, with a furious flurry of rapid-fire notes, like you were being shot in the gut by a machine gun.

My life was never the same after that day. I would walk or hitchhike across Brooklyn, which usually took about an hour, and then knock on his door. Mark never answered the door because he was always in his bedroom in the back of the house, past the living room and kitchen, playing guitar with his door closed. His mom or dad would answer the door politely, invite me in to sit on the couch by the front door, and call out, "Mawwwk, dat kid is here again." Since he was in his early twenties and I was only sixteen—I looked like I was twelve—he really didn't want to have anything to do with me. His parents knew I had walked all the way from Canarsie, though, so they let me sit on the couch in the living room. The thickest dark curtains in the world covered those windows and I would sit there for two or three hours in the dark, hoping Mark might let me in and teach me how to play guitar. Every hour or so, he would have to use the bathroom. So he would walk across the hall from his bedroom, see me sitting there and just shake his head, as if to say, "What is this *kid* doing in my house?"

After a few hours, he would finally invite me in to watch him practice. He practiced almost all day, every day. He lived for music. Ronnie Montrose was like a god to him. His other favorite guitarists were Jimmy Page and Rick Derringer. Whenever he would write or play something original when one of his other guitar-player friends was there, it sounded a lot like something Ronnie or Jimmy would have played. Mark would say, "I was channeling Montrose," or "channeling Jimmy Page."

He hardly spoke to me until I decided to bring my recorder over one day and asked him to put on Jethro Tull's song, "Aqualung." I played along note for note, doing the guitar solo on my flute. He was very surprised and impressed, and said that I "played like a bird. If you could do that on a flute," he said, "then you could also play the guitar." He finally gave me my first lesson, a short blues riff of five notes—the foundation of lead guitar. I went home and practiced the riff over and over, and returned a few days later.

He only made me wait in the dark on the couch in the living room about an hour that day and I thought, *Hey, things are getting better*.

I would watch Mark practice for an hour without him speaking to me, and then he'd show me another blues riff that was four or five notes long. Then he sent me on my way back home.

Whatever he gave me I took very seriously, probably because I had to wait so long for it each time. When I came back, I had it down and played it note-perfect. Eventually, he saw how seriously I took what he taught, and he actually started to talk to me. I became like a little brother to him, and we became friends.

Riot got a record contract and started touring everywhere, just as I went away to college in upstate New York. After a year and a half, I joined a band called Outakontrol in Syracuse in 1979, which perfectly described my life at the time. We later changed our name to Q.T. Hush, the tribute to AC/DC—and I played the part of lead guitarist Angus Young for two years.

By that time Riot's singer had passed away suddenly from cancer and they lost their record deal. I was visiting Brooklyn and called Mark, who said the band was in the studio recording demos to try to get another record deal, He invited me to stop by.

I really don't know why I brought my little recorder along with me that day because by then I was a long-haired, hard rock guitarist who wore black leather jackets. When I arrived they were working on something that was very mellow, almost classical, and it reminded me of the traditional folk song, "Greensleeves." Mark said, "It's too bad you don't have that flute of yours with you. That would have been *great* on this intro."

I said, "I have it in my pocket! I wasn't sure why I brought this with me today. I never bring this anywhere anymore."

So I put on the studio headphones and they recorded me playing a few different variations alongside his classical guitar intro.

A few months later, Riot got a new contract with another major record company. I went to see Mark and he told me the big reason they got signed was because the record company loved the song with the flute intro in it called "Bloodstreets." It started out mellow but then went right into a speed metal frenzy that was very shocking and unique. A music video of that song was made, since it was the band's new single. This video played on the show *Headbanger's Ball* every Saturday night on MTV for three years.

Riot had their time again for a little while; but if it wasn't one problem with them, it was another. Mark asked me to join the group around 1986, but I had just quit the music business the day before and had cut off all of my hair earlier in the day! It was not meant to be.

Twenty years went by, and Mark and I lost contact. In 2010, however, I had the strongest need to reconnect with him and thank him for all he did to teach me about guitar and music. I found a Facebook page called "Riot—The Early Years," that some of the old gang had put together. On it, Mark wrote that his main influence on guitar was George Harrison, no one else. I had been too young to know about George and the Beatles, so I never even knew that Mark was influenced by him.

It took some work to find out Mark was living with his father on Long Island and his battle with Crohn's disease was coming close to an end. I went to visit him and it was great to revisit those old times and memories that we had shared.

Mark passed in January 2012.

Over the past three or so years, since these never-ending coincidences and George's appearances in my life started, I have often wondered when and why this all started. Well, if there's a rock'n' roll heaven, you know they've got one hell of a band up there.

Acknowlegments

I'd like to thank all of my friends all over the world. Since I travel so much, people ask me where my favorite place is, and I always answer, "Wherever I have the most friends."

Thank you to Melanie Camp for helping me to write the first one hundred or so pages of my story and the synopsis back in 2011. I look forward to our next yoga session.

Thank you to Doug Munson for being a great friend, for bringing the idea of St. George to the book, and for pulling everything together for the second hundred or so pages of the book from all of my emails and texts.

Thank you to Bob Friedman for believing that I was telling the truth and publishing this book, as well as pulling it together and overseeing everything. And for coming to Cathy's house party in the first place.

And to my agent, Bill Gladstone, for thinking that someone who had sold a million CDs on his own was worth taking a fifteen-minute phone call from—and then for sending me a contract fifteen minutes later.

To Victoria Sutherland, for letting me stay at her house and for helping me make the connection with Bill.

Thank you to Laurie Pentell for the excellent copy-editing.

And to Anthony Pomes of Square One Publishers, who went over the book with the excellent eye of an inspired editor and a Beatles historian.

To Robert Murray, author of *The Stars Still Shine*. I made contact with Bob while this book was being completed. His friendship and help have been invaluable to me in understanding this process. He has a big role in Book 2.

Namasté to all.

I would like to thank the gift of music for keeping me company all my life and to God, The Source, the great positive force in life that has shown me a way to keep making a living with music, so I can continue to be creative.

And I would like to thank George for all of the obvious reasons.

I would especially like to thank my mom, Sandy. I had been telling her all of these things as they happened and about three months before the book was finished, I asked her if she truly believed everything. She said, "Yes, I have to."

My mom was a para-professional teacher in a vocational high school in Brooklyn, New York. Her job was to take students with learning disabilities who couldn't pass and help them so they could graduate. She treated all of them like they were her own kids and had the highest success rate in New York City history. She helped change the lives of countless people who were then able to get their diplomas so they could get a better job, and have a better life.

It's kind of funny that the one thing she has always said to me during hard times was, "This too shall pass." I think that's as close to *All Things Must Pass* as you can get.

There's a lot I could say about my mom but instead, I will share with you what all of the teachers who worked beside her at different times over the past thirty or so years wrote as a goodbye letter to her at her retirement party on February 16, 2007:

To a tiny woman who has the biggest heart in the world
Who keeps herself busy making other peoples' lives easier
Who always has a good word to
say to someone that needs it most
Whose laughter is infectious
Who brings cheer to a lonely soul
Who teaches people how to make sense of life
no matter how senseless things can be
We wish you the happiest birthday
and a enjoyable retirement,
From the teachers of Grady High School

About the Author

David Young has recorded more than 50 albums and has sold over a million CDs. His relaxing instrumental music features his unique technique of playing two recorders (renaissance flutes) in harmony at the same time. Some have called his music "The most beautiful music on Earth."

He is also an accomplished singer/songwriter/guitarist whose voice and songs have been used on numerous TV productions. His arrangement of the Joni Mitchell song, "Woodstock," from his musical *The Mystery of Destiny*, was used for the 40th Anniversary of the Woodstock festival exhibit at the Newseum in Washington, D.C.

His new genre of "Musical Affirmations," which features one healing mantra that is sung and blended into each one-hour CD, have been used by numerous psychotherapists and were featured at the American Psychological Association National Convention in 2013.

His album *Christmas Morning* by Celestial Winds (an earlier group) was the number-two album on the charts in Canada in November-December 1994.

His made-for-TV movie, *Village of Dreams* (filmed in Rothenburg, Germany), has been played on TV over 400 times in America.

Over 10,000 massage therapists, spas, healing centers, and hospitals throughout the world use his instrumental music every day to help people find peace in this stressful world.

Special Offers

To the readers who have had experiences with loved ones who have passed, but with whom you still feel a special connection: If you have stories you would like to share about those experiences, please send them to:

David Young Music
Heaven on Earth Productions
270-F North El Camino Real #485
Encinitas, CA 92024

To download three free instrumental songs from my *Yoga Soundtrack* CD as a gift for purchasing this book, go to:
www.davidyoungmusic.com/yoga3

To download three free songs from the *Rock'n'Soul* soundtrack CD, which has songs from this story, go to:
www.davidyoungmusic.com/rocknsoul3

There are two soundtrack CDs that can be purchased as companions of this book. One is an instrumental CD called *Channeling Harrison Yoga Soundtrack*. The other is a vocal CD that features all of the songs shared in this story, and it's called *Channeling Harrison Vocal Soundtrack*. If you purchase one of these, you will receive the other as a free gift just by entering the code 999. You can find them at:
www.davidyoungmusic.com

To order a 12" by 18" full color poster of the front cover, please send $12 plus $4 postage and handling to the address above.

Related Titles

If you enjoyed *Channeling Harrison,* you may also enjoy
other Rainbow Ridge titles. Read more about them at
www.rainbowridgebooks.com.

The Cosmic Internet: Explanations from the Other Side
by Frank DeMarco

Dance of the Electric Hummingbird
by Patricia Walker

Coming Full Circle: Ancient Teachings for a Modern World
by Lynn Andrews

*Afterlife Conversations with Hemingway: A Dialogue on
His Life, His Work and the Myth*
by Frank DeMarco

*Consciousness: Bridging the Gap between Conventional Science
and the New Super Science of Quantum Mechanics*
by Eva Herr

Messiah's Handbook: Reminders for the Advanced Soul
by Richard Bach

Blue Sky, White Clouds
by Eliezer Sobel

Inner Vegas: Creating Miracles, Abundance, and Health
by Joe Gallenberger

When the Horses Whisper
by Rosalyn Berne

Your Soul Remembers
by Joanne DiMaggio

Rainbow Ridge Books publishes spiritual, metaphysical, and self-help titles, and is distributed by Square One Publishers in Garden City Park, New York.

To contact authors and editors, peruse our titles, and see submission guidelines, please visit our website at

www.rainbowridgebooks.com